# DIVERSITY, EQUITY, AND INCLUSION IN THE WORKPLACE

### DEVELOPING DEI SOLUTIONS

KIM WILSON

© **Copyright 2023 - All rights reserved.**

The content contained within this book may not be reproduced, duplicated or transmitted without direct written permission from the author or the publisher.

Under no circumstances will any blame or legal responsibility be held against the publisher, or author, for any damages, reparation, or monetary loss due to the information contained within this book, either directly or indirectly.

Legal Notice:

This book is copyright protected. It is only for personal use. You cannot amend, distribute, sell, use, quote or paraphrase any part, or the content within this book, without the consent of the author or publisher.

Disclaimer Notice:

Please note the information contained within this document is for educational and entertainment purposes only. All effort has been executed to present accurate, up to date, reliable, complete information. No warranties of any kind are declared or implied. Readers acknowledge that the author is not engaged in the rendering of legal, financial, medical or professional advice. The content within this book has been derived from various sources. Please consult a licensed professional before attempting any techniques outlined in this book.

By reading this document, the reader agrees that under no circumstances is the author responsible for any losses, direct or indirect, that are incurred as a result of the use of the information contained within this document, including, but not limited to, errors, omissions, or inaccuracies.

# CONTENTS

*Introduction*   7
*About the Author*   11

1. GETTING TO KNOW DIVERSITY, EQUITY, AND INCLUSION   13
   Introduction to Diversity, Equity, and Inclusion   14
   Difference From Traditional Employee Management   27
   Importance of DEI in the Workplace   31

2. HIT THE RESET BUTTON ON BIAS   37
   Types of Unconscious Bias   38
   Recognizing and Responding to Bias   44
   Techniques for Modifying Behavior, Policies, and Practices   48
   Creating a More Equitable Workplace Environment   51

3. HOW MUCH IS IT COSTING YOUR COMPANY NOT TO HAVE A DEI STRATEGY?   55
   Costs of Not Having a DEI Strategy   56
   The ROI of Investing in a DEI Strategy   59

4. DIVERSITY IN THE WORKPLACE — CORPORATE AMERICA'S OVERDUE FACELIFT   63
   The Ansira Case   64
   Autism at Work by SAP   65
   TransFocus at Mozilla   66
   Female Leaders at Verizon   67

| | |
|---|---|
| Be Yourself at Johnson & Johnson | 68 |
| In Other Words | 69 |
| **5. HOW DEI BENEFITS BOTTOM LINES** | **71** |
| The Financial Benefits of DEI | 72 |
| The Impact of DEI on Business Performance | 75 |
| Creating a Sustainable Competitive Advantage Through DEI Initiatives | 78 |
| **6. BUILDING A DEI FRAMEWORK** | **83** |
| Initiating and Leading Employee Resource Groups | 86 |
| Building a Diversified Internal Pipeline for People Managers and Leadership Positions | 89 |
| **7. TAKING THE PULSE OF YOUR COMPANY'S CULTURE** | **95** |
| Measuring Engagement | 99 |
| Identifying Areas for Improvement | 101 |
| Creating Action Plans to Drive Change and Improve Performance | 102 |
| **8. FINDING CHAMPIONS** | **105** |
| The Role of DEI Champions | 105 |
| Leading Employee Resource Groups to Advance DEI Initiatives | 108 |
| **9. WHAT TO INCLUDE IN YOUR DEI TRAINING AND INITIATIVES** | **111** |
| Designing DEI Training Programs | 113 |
| Inculcating a Culture of Acceptance and Respect | 115 |
| Using Technology to Enhance Learning Experiences | 118 |
| **10. TIME TO SPREAD THE WORD** | **121** |
| Eight Ways to Promote and Communicate Your DEI Framework | 122 |

11. HOW TO CHANGE MINDS FROM THE
    GROUND LEVEL TO THE C-SUITE                131
    Engaging Managers and the C-Suite in
    DEI Initiatives                             132
    Empowering Employees to Lead Change         135

12. "ARE WE THERE YET?" — TRACKING
    YOUR PROGRESS                               141
    Setting Measurable Goals                    142
    Using Data to Create Actionable Insights    148
    Ensuring Accountability for Results         150

13. CELEBRATING SUCCESS                         153
    Recognizing Achievements                    154
    Creating Meaningful Ways to
    Acknowledge Progress                        156
    Encourage Employee Participation and
    Engagement                                  159

14. SIX COMMON MISTAKES LEADERS
    MAKE WITH DEI INITIATIVES                   161
    Mistake #1: Not Taking DEI Seriously        162
    Mistake #2: Not Involving Stakeholders
    and Partners in Planning Process            164
    Mistake #3: Failing to Prioritize All
    Elements of DEI                             165
    Mistake #4: Ignoring the Importance of
    Inclusion and Intersectionality             166
    Mistake #5: Inadequate Training and
    Resources                                   168
    Mistake #6: Lack of Accountability and
    Follow-Through                              169
    In Other Words                              170

15. THE WORKPLACE DEI CHECKLIST                 173
    Conducting a DEI Audit                      174
    DEI Checklist                               175

*Conclusion* 181
*References* 187

# INTRODUCTION

> *Good leadership requires you to surround yourself with people of diverse perspectives who can disagree with you without fear of retaliation.*
>
> — DORIS KEARNS GOODWIN

According to data from McKinsey (2022), 70% of companies believe diversity, equity, and inclusion (DEI) efforts are "extremely critical." Yet, only 34% of organizations have enough resources to implement DEI initiatives (Corrigan, 2022). In a world that has constantly been demanding the increase in the participation of minorities in the workplace, implementing DEI in a company can be challenging. This does not mean that the efforts have not been made—they have.

According to a recent survey, 94% of employers and 74% of employees affirmed that the company they work for has made an effort to advance the initiative (Fenelon et al., 2022).

However, making these programs successful is another story. The same survey claims that while companies seem committed to implementing a DEI program, only 49% of the employees agreed that the initiative had clear goals. In addition, one in every four people claimed that they were unsure of the organization's progress regarding the programs. But why does this happen? Does it come from an ineffective implementation of the DEI framework, or are these companies simply failing to communicate their efforts to their employees and the general public?

If you are reading this book and are in a leadership or HR role, you have likely faced the same challenges as others in implementing an effective DEI initiative. You may want to polish up your knowledge of implementing it in your company or find a strategy that will work and produce results. No matter the reason, you probably aim to find a solution to address the DEI issues in your organization and produce results that go beyond hiring people of a specific group just to make a visible impact.

If you have just been promoted as a leader in your organization, this might be the challenge you have been given—bringing change to the workplace. Your company might not have started putting a DEI initiative in place, or the current one might need revision. Maybe the framework or the policy that has been set is causing internal and external conflict due to the lack of a comprehensive approach. Perhaps the policy that has been established only considers the minimum of what can be done and was established only so that the company can say that they have something in place. In this case, you are looking for reliable resources you can use to help formulate a plan for creating and implementing DEI programs, policies, and initiatives within your company. Last but not least, you might need to justify budget issues and increases for DEI applications.

## HOW WILL THIS BOOK HELP?

Regardless of the reason, you have come to this book looking for help—and I am here to help and guide you through implementing an effective DEI initiative in your company. One of the things that we will do is learn how to recognize and reduce unconscious bias in your own DEI planning. By reading this book, you will be given the tools to develop your framework—here, you won't be given a pre-fabricated solution. You will learn to set up one that matches your organization's core beliefs, mission, and values. You will learn how to change the mindset of employees at all levels of the organization and avoid making the most common mistakes.

Speaking of mistakes when implementing a DEI framework; do you know what the most common ones are? According to WellRight (2022), they include a need for more goals and metrics, inadequate training, low or no prioritization by leadership, budgetary restrictions, and cultural resistance. Do any or all of these, ring a bell in your head? Can you identify where your organization needs to improve? If you have, rest assured that every one of these items will be addressed in this book, and I will bring you solutions so that these problems are solved. Once you finish reading, you will have a clear plan to implement the DEI initiative in your company and promote and communicate it internally and externally.

# ABOUT THE AUTHOR

My name is Kim, and I have worked in human resources for several companies throughout my career. I have spent a considerable number of years working with large organizations and helping them empower their employees to grow and successfully attain business key performance indicators (KPIs). Today, my main focus is to help companies implement effective DEI initiatives and guide them through the steps needed to succeed. My main objective is to give fellow leaders and managers, working in HR, an easy-to-understand guide on DEI that can help them walk through the steps of planning and implementing programs within their organizations.

# 1

## GETTING TO KNOW DIVERSITY, EQUITY, AND INCLUSION

> *Every individual matters. Every individual has a role to play. Every individual makes a difference.*
>
> — JANE GOODALL

Why do companies struggle to effectively put DEI strategies in place? Although I could write an extensive list of reasons for this, I want to focus on what I believe is the main issue: reading and writing about it is easier than its implementation. *Why?* You might ask. The answer is simple: While some people tend to understand and tolerate that people are different, they struggle to understand why some people need to be placed within a framework of inclusion.

These people simply do not understand that struggles because of gender, race, physical abilities, or any other possible cause for marginalization, are historical and have even led to wars throughout history. According to Shufeldt (2021), if differences that we have with others —cultural and otherwise—haven't been solved in centuries of human existence, why would it be different in the workplace?

## INTRODUCTION TO DIVERSITY, EQUITY, AND INCLUSION

To understand how different each of us are, we need to think of ourselves as a bowl of soup (Killermann, 2012). Our "base and broth" are composed of our essential traits: race, ethnicity, gender, sexuality, and ability status. From this, we need to enhance the recipe with the "early additions," which are our socioeconomic status, geographical location, education, and family structure. The "optional ingredients" are based on those that come with our character and upbringing: hobbies and passions, religion and faith, as well as career and political beliefs. Finally, to perfect the soup, we will add the "secret ingredients," which are the experiences we have had throughout our life.

Now, if you think of it this way, although we might share some common "ingredients," it is pretty safe to say that there is no "soup" similar to another—much as there is no person that is exactly the same. Even if you are identical twins, your life experiences will be different than those of the other; therefore, this will make what you are "composed of" different. Likewise, a person who is white and from a wealthy family will probably have a different view on life than one who is black and is from a less-wealthy family. Independent of the situation, this does not make anyone else's stories invalid or false—they are just different. This is an integral part of your *identity*.

Even though some people have the prefabricated speech that "we are all humans" or "everyone is equal," we know this is not true. Due to bias or preconceived ideas, some people have fewer opportunities than others. This includes all those not part of the white, cis, and heterosexual men group. How often have you seen pictures of company management composed of people with these characteristics and asked yourself: *What about women? People of a different ethnicity? Those with disabilities?* This is not as unusual as you might think. However, groups fighting for minority rights and society, in general, have started demanding change—*now*. According to Winder (2022),

> Today, the employee and the employer must be on the same page about the fact that the color of

one's skin, their position on the socioeconomic scale and the gender spectrum or even the level of ability cannot exclude an individual who rightfully deserves the position (p. 4).

And this is precisely where a diversity, equity, and inclusion program factors in.

### Definition of DEI

While some people might understand what diversity, equity, and inclusion mean, defining their specific application in human resources is critical. When we talk about *diversity*, we refer to the characteristics, similarities, and differences in a team or group that cannot be measured, such as age, gender, language, race, and religious commitment. Diversity refers to the differences among people and what makes each of them unique and can be originated at birth or from the person's life experience.

*Inclusion* refers to a set of practices that an organization will implement to ensure employees feel safe. It will also make them feel that they "belong" and are respected independently of the group they belong to. When the company practices inclusion, the employees feel welcome and, at some level, comfortable working in that place because they feel they can be themselves without needing to hide or be ashamed. Inclusion will allow people from different backgrounds and distinct characteristics to work together as a team, accepting each other as they are.

When we talk about *equity*, it means that the process, or processes, will be carried out without bias in an impartial manner so that every person has a chance. This means that the process will be carried out to ensure that a team is diverse and that populations or groups are represented as much as possible. By applying equity, the company will remove partiality from the selection process, and the process will be fair to all, independent of their characteristics. Equity within the workplace will lead to *equality*. And how are these different? Read along to find out.

**Equity vs. Equality**

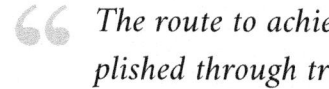

> *The route to achieving equity will not be accomplished through treating everyone equally. It will be achieved by treating everyone justly according to their circumstances.*
>
> — PAULA DRESSEL, RACE MATTERS INSTITUTE

Although equity and equality may seem like similar words, they are not. To illustrate the example, let's suppose we are talking about a group of people, all of which are different. When we talk about *equality*, it means giving all the people that belong to this group access to the same opportunities without considering their specific needs. Therefore, even though the company might be acting in what they believe is each person's best interest, some people will remain excluded since the solution that was proposed to the group did not apply to them. In equality, the phrase "one size fits all" can be used, although it is not practical.

However, if we consider the same group of people and apply *equity*, we will be thinking about the specific needs of those who belong to it. When we talk about equity, it means that the tools and opportunities are distributed among those in the group so that everyone has the same opportunity. In this case, the solutions are personalized and adapted so that each individual is given the resources to have the same opportunity as the other based on their needs.

Based on the explanation above, it is possible to identify where most companies go wrong—while most of them are promoting equality, what they really want is to provide more opportunities for equity. Can you think of examples of when this has happened? Maybe this happens in your organization or others you have already worked for. Sometimes, although with the best intentions, organizations put in place equality practices without considering the specific needs of certain members of the organization. Therefore, despite their best efforts, its members still have differences. For that reason, one of the first things you should consider when implementing a DEI action is: How does this solution enable the individuals in the workplace?

## *Origins of DEI*

Despite DEI initiatives becoming more popular recently due to social movements, efforts to promote inclusion in the workplace have existed for at least 80 years. One of the first attempts toward diminishing discrimination in the United States came from Executive Order 8802, signed by President Roosevelt in 1941. The order determined that "there would be no discrimination in the U.S. defense industry based on race, color, or national origin" (Murray, 2019) and established the Fair Employment Practices Committee (FEPC). Now, you have to remember that this was during World War II, and people were already suffering from unemployment that was not military-related. Even where there were jobs, African Americans were subjected to discrimination in government-related positions. To avoid popular manifestations, the president's reaction was to sign the order.

Shortly after the war ended and President Truman took office, he signed an executive order to guarantee equal rights in the workplace between employees from different races. However, this order did not forbid segregation. As a result, African American soldiers were able to enlist in the army; however, they were still subject to discrimination. This effort to avoid segregation was achieved in 1948 and is considered by some scholars as "the first diversity initiative in the workplace" (McCormick, 2007). However, although efforts were made, there was still a lack of diversity in the workplaces that continued to be dominated by white men. While no action was taken, social pressure continued to grow as women and people from other ethnicities wanted to occupy their positions in corporations.

In 1960, things began to change with the efforts made regarding affirmative action and non-discrimination. Some legislation passed to enforce these rights and guarantee an equal workplace include the Equal Pay Act of 1963, Title VIII of the Civil Rights Act of 1964, and the Age Discrimination in Employment Act of 1967. Each of these acts targeted a distinct obstacle in the workplace—different pay between men and women who performed the same function, inability to obtain a job due to race, color, religion, or sex, as well as discrimination against those who were aged over 40 and were looking for job placement. Although well-intentioned, breaking these laws only demanded training for the companies rather than demanding that they enforce the practice.

Once these acts were signed, minimal progress was made regarding diversity and inclusion in the 1980s, when the lack of diversity in the workplace became evident. Social pressure played its part, and the government and Fortune 500 companies saw themselves in a place where they had to help minorities successfully enter the workplace. The focus, however, was still on a compliance manner rather than effectively having a diverse approach. Anand and Winters (2008) state that although more women were being hired in the period, it was visible that they were not growing in their careers and were being given fewer opportunities than men–without mentioning the lower pay they were offered. For budgetary reasons, companies and the government reduced diversity training and initiatives, which was reflected in the groups that organizations hired. What they were not expecting, however, was an increase in the number of immigrants arriving in the country, the number of people retiring, and the desire of the new generation to see changes in the workplace.

In the early 1990s, companies struggled to see affirmative action produce any results; thus, their goals were not being achieved. But in a shift of thought, companies soon started worrying about how their products and services reflected the diverse characteristics of their target markets. The words "social justice" began to be heard, and companies wanted to reflect the changes that society was demanding. This led to organizations conducting "sensitivity and awareness" training sessions. At the same time, universities and scholars started writing articles on diversity, the lack of inclusion, and the impact that this had on society. Although there was a change in how things should work, diversity was still viewed as a "problem," especially for the homogenous mass that dominated the companies, which was mostly still made up of white, cis, heterosexual men. Instead of these men thinking about ways to improve their corporate environment, they were placed in a situation in which they should be feeling "guilty" about not being inclusive, leading to the birth of terms and concepts such as "backlash" and "reverse discrimination" (Anand & Winters, 2008).

The landscape started to change in the 2000s when organizations began to see that having a diverse workplace benefits them and creates a positive brand image in the eyes of the public. Companies began hiring people from different minority groups, and diversity became an essential value to leaders and managers. Inclusivity initiatives became a standard in organizations that began seeing people with different characteristics on their boards and in management positions. Pictures of company management and employees were further away from all-white men, and more diversity was observed. Human resources departments began transforming into employee resource groups (ERGs), and new steps have been taken that strive to travel further than adhering to compliance.

As initiatives continue to grow, the DEI framework is established, companies start directing more budget toward it, and a more diverse environment is created. To illustrate the point, let me give you a few numbers on how much things changed at this time. By the beginning of the year 2000, 60% of the women in the United States were employed, composing 39.49% of the global workforce—the number remained similar in 2018, with 57.1% of the women currently in the workplace and composing 38.85% of the workforce (VSource, 2020). The efforts within the companies continue, and as DEI initiatives increase, we will likely see more people from minority groups becoming part of the workforce. I could say that just buying and reading this book is already a step forward!

## Implementing DEI—A Business Case

You might be asking yourself: *Why would I work on DEI, and what is the business case for my company?* My answer to you could be quite simple because corporate social responsibility is the right thing to do, regardless of how complex implementing DEI will directly impact your business sales, reputation, and market share, among others. The key here is that the people involved in the decision-making within the organization understand that putting a DEI framework in place is not just "because they have to." Setting DEI objectives needs to go further than placing a plan on paper so that it will look good. It needs to be sewn within the company's values and objectives to be something the organization believes in and wants to work toward.

This is the main issue you need to consider when implementing a DEI project: You will need to study and engage the stakeholders to have a positive outcome. The participation of the internal and external stakeholders in the process will be essential to ascertain the success of your idea. There is no use in having human resources do the research, build a framework, and organize campaigns if there will be no involvement from the organization's leaders, for example.

Georgeac & Rattan (2022) define a business case for diversity as "a rhetoric that justifies diversity in the workplace because it benefits companies' bottom line." For this reason, establishing a DEI initiative needs to be linked to the company's key objectives and values that they present to the public. This means that your final determination will need to be considered in the organization's plans, future goals, provided services, and offered products. To do this, the first step of the process is to speak to the company management and establish the following:

- What changes do you want to make, and where should they be carried out?
- Does the company leadership agree with implementing the program and is committed to making it work?
- The need to assess where the company could improve its DEI initiative and to what extent it can make changes.
- If you have the authorization to speak to other branches or offices, in the case of global companies, to get their input on the different views according to the location's culture.

Before going to management, you should have conducted thorough research. Anticipate the questions that might be asked and the relevant answers thereof. My main suggestion is to develop the presentation intended for the management and stakeholders, by providing context to the situation and showing how placing a DEI initiative will help the company improve and profit. You need to show you understand the reality of minorities, including the demographics and differences between them and the general population. This will ensure more credibility to your presentation and allow you to be in a place where you can request that action be taken.

The final thing to remember when building your business case is that diversity is more than gender, race, or age. It includes several other minorities that, most of the time, are not considered. McKim (2021) reminds us what implementing a DEI framework is all about: "realize that DEI is all about people. I suggest you consider DEI as an organizational approach or set of principles rather than a goal or objective. DEI should be in the DNA of your organization—in everything your employees do."

## DIFFERENCE FROM TRADITIONAL EMPLOYEE MANAGEMENT

When you consider implementing a DEI initiative, you will see how the manner in which the company manages employees will need to change. This generally means that there will be a shift from traditional management to more strategic leadership. Before the arrival of a new form of HR management, companies used to see the department as a place where employee compliance was to be held together with efficient record keeping, payments, and hiring solutions. While following rules and practices are still part of the job description, so are making decisions that will impact the corporation's strategy going forward, including organizational development. Suffice it to say that when speaking of development, a new DEI approach ought to be included.

The HR department is now responsible for more than the traditional "pushing paper"—their focus has turned to be, first and foremost, what its name suggests: *humans*. Imagine what would have happened during the COVID-19 pandemic if these departments were not flexible when everyone changed from an office to a remote work setting. This included needing to be more empathetic toward the other's situation, which often had children interrupting, homeschooling needs, and many others. The HR departments were required to adjust company policies, culture, and views, including using new technology and adapting work hours. While some companies insist on maintaining the same procedures and using limited software that manages numbers, newer developments have been made so that people can be seen.

Formality is also something that has changed entirely. Remember when feedback on performance used to be done once a year with a scheduled time and place? Well, that's all in the past. One of the main reasons for this is that 85% of millennials, the new workforce, think they would be more effective if they had more feedback sessions throughout the year (Milligan, 2017). Not only this, but according to JazzHR (2021), 90% of HR leaders are not satisfied with how the performance reviews are carried out in the companies they work for, claiming they need more context and that contributions are summarized and minimized.

Milligan (2017) makes a meaningful prediction. According to the author, "The HR of the next decade has to be more focused on performance and productivity. And that's going to require a seismic shift in thinking." Thinking along the same lines, this is precisely what having a DEI approach will bring to organizations. It will leave the approach of something that companies should have to become an essential item if they want to stand out from other organizations.

### *How Is DEI Different?*

Let's go back to the previous section, where COVID-19 and the changes incurred in the workplace are mentioned. Can you think about the changes that happened within your organization? Or maybe the changes that occurred in companies where people you know work? How were people affected? What changed in their priorities and the way they see work?

One of the things that has changed is access to social media. Mostly everyone you know has it, and consequently, companies are susceptible to dealing with public opinion more often than not. Remember when I mentioned the corporate picture of all-white men in suits representing the company's management? How would this image be seen if posted on social media, especially by activists for minorities? It is safe to say that no company wants to undergo the scrutiny that comes with the public judging what their board looks like. And even if they try hiring actors for billboards and corporate pictures, for example, it is possible that the backlash they receive from social media would be even more damaging if the truth were to be uncovered. Although most companies still restrict access on corporate computers to these types of channels, they are slowly coming to realize that this is how new generations communicate and that disallowing them to do so will create discomfort in the workplace. Of course, this does not mean that companies are starting to allow employees the full 40 hours on Facebook or Instagram, however, some have become more lenient regarding the matter.

More generally, companies use their financial power to impact and provoke change in the American scenario. Giants such as McDonald's are creating initiatives such as low-interest loans to have more diverse franchise owners. Others are giving a percentage of their supplier and vendor contracts to companies that apply a DEI initiative or to companies owned by minorities. More organizations are creating ERG groups focused on minorities, while decision-makers and leaders are taking a unique role in promoting them and keeping them alive. The more you look around, the more obvious it becomes to see how DEI is changing the actions of traditional corporations.

Last, we must consider that employees are becoming the demanding part of the equation. Whether it is because they want a more diverse environment or because they analyze their options before taking a job, they have been some of the propellers of change. For instance, women now want workspaces to be flexible regarding their needs if they have children. Disabled individuals look for work where they feel they will have support for their specific needs. Members of the LGBTQIAP+ avoid working with companies that do not embrace a diverse approach to the workplace. The examples go on and on.

Major players in the market hold town halls with employees specifically on the DEI theme. DEI is being integrated into the onboarding of new teams. Access to training is being given to all with an equal opportunity. DEI is modifying the way management works. It is changing how leaders think about and approach present and future employees by listening—to HR, employees, stakeholders, and especially the public.

## IMPORTANCE OF DEI IN THE WORKPLACE

It is undeniable that implementing a DEI program in your company will bring benefits in the short and long term. It is proven to be incredibly successful when all stakeholders are involved and the leadership is active. Organizations have started to observe improvement in several areas where this has been implemented: The overhead is lower, motivation is higher, profits and production go up, and the public responds well. If you think that this is still something that needs to gain momentum and importance, here are a few numbers discussed by Buss (2022) relating to DEI initiatives in American corporations:

> Over the last year, the most frequent action taken by companies on the DEI front has been to conduct DEI-focused "employee listening," such as surveys and focus groups, with 47% of respondents to a recent survey by the American Productivity & Quality Center executing such moves. Also, 36% increased staff dedicated to DEI; 32% increased their DEI budgets; 31% "established new avenues for reporting DEI complaints;" and 30% each had disclosed DEI metrics publicly and invested more in employee resource and affinity groups (p. 10).

After looking at these numbers, I think you can see that DEI is here to stay—it has become an essential element for companies considering continuing their businesses in the future. But where does the shift begin? Where is the starting point of the action? What is the most significant aspect of the company that changes for this to be true? The answer to these questions is in only one word: culture.

## *Creating a Positive Culture*

When you integrate DEI into the company's workplace, you are committing to include it in its core values. This contemplates applying it from the hiring process and seeing it through all the way to customer service and product delivery. But it is not only about the final product; inclusion goes way beyond this. Think about something as simple as your company's dress code. How does it affect people from different genders and religions? Does it segregate people who dress differently than what the "common" person wears? If the answer is yes, then a change is needed.

Applying the framework means that employees will feel like they belong, increasing productivity and performance levels. Once you decide to include DEI in the workplace, employees will feel that the company understands them and their journey—enhancing engagement and diminishing problems with harassment and discrimination. Going back to the dress code example, imagine the positive impact of accepting traditional clothing or outfits respecting others' religions would mean on your employees. Considering their beliefs, traditions, and rituals would most certainly make them feel safe in the workplace. A slight shift in culture would go a long way toward DEI initiatives.

But due to this, you will have to work with communication. In this sense, I mean communication that goes both ways: top-down and bottom-up. When you implement DEI in your organization, you will create a culture of listening to what employees say. Because you listen to them, they will feel more recognized and prioritized. Listening what they need means facilitating dialogue, creating programs to encourage talent, and removing bias from processes so that it is fair to all. Some companies even implement mentorship with senior members to help develop employee development.

These practices, which can include many others, will lead to changes in company culture. Instead of having a culture of oppression and discrimination, you will create a positive culture for those working there. However, this means performing a complete 180-degree turnaround in the company's practices and processes. It is not only about creating guides and committing to change, it is about actually implementing them. Once you see the impacts of a positive culture on employee behavior, such as an increase in morale and lower turnover, you will likely ask yourself why you didn't do this before.

Creating an equitable and inclusive workplace by implementing a DEI framework will bring changes to your organization—that is a fact. As more companies address the issue, leadership will start steering away from traditional management styles and embracing change and diversity. Employees' voices will be heard, and a culture of respect and acceptance that reflects other aspects of society will be seen. Remember that the main issue is to listen to the stakeholders to ensure a more equitable and diverse environment.

The starting point? It all begins with a change in mindset—challenging your assumptions and removing any unconscious bias you or others within the organization might have. This can be done by enhancing communication, carrying out training sessions, and providing information. Let's move on to the following chapter to determine some actions that can be taken to understand and re-evaluate your view on bias.

# 2

## HIT THE RESET BUTTON ON BIAS

If you are still in doubt about the need to implement DEI in your company, you should know that companies that have more diversity tend to have better financial performances (Hunt et al., 2015). Although this does not mean that diversity will automatically translate into profit within your organization, a large majority of companies that are successful implemented a diversity framework. Do you see a pattern here?

Before we jump into the different types of bias and those affected, I propose an exercise. Suppose that you have two candidates for a job opening. One is fresh out of college and the other is over 50. Traditional practices will suggest that the younger candidate will have more energy and will be able to dedicate themselves more to the job because they likely do not have a family and could spend more time working without other worries. On the other hand, the older candidate might be considered to have an "expiry date" and old-fashioned.

If these are the first thoughts you have when you see both resumes in front of you, I'm sorry to be the one to say this, but you are being biased. You might not have considered that the older candidate has more industry experience that could give the company a competitive advantage. It is very likely that they might have an extensive client portfolio built through their years in the market. If you choose to discard this, or other candidates, for reasons that go beyond the competencies and their skills, even if you are doing it unconsciously, you are practicing unconscious bias.

## TYPES OF UNCONSCIOUS BIAS

Suppose you have another opening for a position in your company. After interviewing several candidates, you decide to hire the one that appeals more to your "gut instincts." Whether you know this or not, you are probably acting on an unconscious or implicit bias. Wilson (2021) defines unconscious bias as "what happens when we act on subconscious, deeply ingrained biases, stereotypes, and attitudes formed from our inherent human cognition, experiences, upbringing, and environment." This type of attitude, even if not on purpose, can negatively affect a company because of procedures carried out during the hiring process or their daily operations.

Bias is different from discrimination; the main difference is that, while the first is not against the law, the second is. This is because bias happens unconsciously, and we generally carry it out without being aware of what we are doing. It might be implicit in how you speak, the clothes you choose, or the places you go without noticing. On the other hand, if you are consciously making these decisions and are behaving with bad intentions, you are being discriminative. Unconscious bias is much more challenging to identify than discrimination because people practice it without realizing it. Let's take a look at ten examples of bias.

1. **Ageism**—This type of bias happens when there are negative feelings toward a person because of their age. This may involve receiving fewer work opportunities or different treatment from colleagues because of age. According to Urwin (2019), "62 percent of workers 50 and above believe older workers face age discrimination, but over 93 percent assert that ageism in the workplace is a regular occurrence".
2. **Gender bias**—Women tend to be more affected than men with this type of bias. Researchers

identified that men are 1.5 times more likely to occupy an open position or receive a promotion in the workplace when compared to women with the same abilities (Issid, 2011). Although this type of discrimination is prohibited under the Civil Rights Act, this does not stop it from happening, with women being treated less favorably compared to male colleagues and candidates.

3. **Affinity bias**—When people favor those most similar to them—in behavior, values, thoughts, backgrounds, and actions—they are committing affinity bias. For example, this will happen in the workplace when they believe that a candidate will be a "better fit" to the culture than the other. This is one of the most common biases in the workplace, and "while similarities shouldn't automatically disqualify a candidate, they should never be the deciding factor, either" (Xu, 2019).

4. **Confirmation bias**—If you have ever seen an opportunity where the company is hiring only candidates that have been to a specific list of universities, for example, you should know that they are practicing confirmation bias. In this type of bias, the organization has a preconceived idea about something or a

situation that they believe is true, even if they do not have the information to confirm their belief. This can also occur depending on a person's region, name, and other attributes that might be presented in the CV without getting to know the candidate first.

5. **Beauty bias**—In a type of bias that affects both men and women, beauty bias occurs when a company thinks that an individual's capabilities are more or less significant based on their attractiveness. This is independent of race, and it seems to make employers feel that those who are more attractive, are more successful than those who are not. If you still think this does not exist, a 2018 study by Lee et al. found that "when selecting for the desirable job, 62.89% of participants selected the attractive individual." On the other hand, attractive people can be discriminated against for roles that companies feel are "beneath" them.

6. **Halo effect**—When hiring, looking for items where the candidate stands out or seems to have the best accomplishment is common. However, a halo effect bias occurs once this candidate is placed on a pedestal because of a particular characteristic or background event. This can happen within any part of the hiring

process—looking at a person's merits is still something companies do during the selection process. When evaluating a candidate, the hiring team favors the one who seems to have the best results and does not consider the opportunities that the other candidates might have had.

7. **Name bias**—Suppose the company is conducting a hiring process and receives two resumes: One under the name John Smith and the other with the name José Santos. Suppose the option of the organization is to interview the first but not the second because of the subconscious implication of a different background that can be seen in the name. In that case, they are committing name bias. Studies have shown that "distinctively black names reduce the probability of employer contact by 2.1 percentage points relative to distinctively white names" (Kline et al., 2021).

8. **Nonverbal bias**—People communicate with their bodies. How often have you heard someone say this or been coached to observe the other's body language to interpret what they *really* mean? Unfortunately, this can lead to a type of bias where the candidate is judged because of the firmness of their handshake,

whether or not they can hold eye contact, or even if they smile. This type of bias does not consider that people are different, and this might not impact their productivity or skills—it could just be nerves about undergoing the hiring process or extreme shyness.

9. **Authority bias**—Although this type of bias does not happen during the interview phase, it is one of the most common to identify in the workplace. Suppose a problem needs to be solved, and a junior employee proposes an alternative solution. The idea might be immediately dismissed while, if the same proposal was made by one of the bosses or leaders, it would be accepted. This is a type of authority bias where the company only listens to those higher up in the hierarchy, even if it's not the best decision for the organization. A study published in 2019 stated that 60% of the employees in the interviewed companies identified authority bias often or always within their organization (Mignot, 2020).

10. **Weight bias**—People with high body weight have a less probable chance of being hired when compared to those who have lower body weight, independent of gender. What is worse, studies affirm that these professionals earn

lower wages, where obese women earn 6% less than their thinner counterparts, while this happens to 3% of men (Rudd Center, 2020). These professionals are also seen as less competent and less productive, in addition to several other negative stereotypes.

While I have outlined a list with a few examples, other types of bias are still possible. But what should a company do to recognize and respond to these types of bias? How can this be avoided? What choices can organizations make to change these unconscious biases that have become a structural part of their processes?

RECOGNIZING AND RESPONDING TO BIAS

The first thing that needs to be done to effectively combat unconscious bias is identifying it. This means going over procedures and standards within the organization to see if it is practiced in a personal or institutional manner. You can identify this by conducting surveys, observing the workplace, and reviewing previous hiring processes and current promotions. Doing so will enable you to understand where your company is going wrong and what needs improvement. Keeping records of recent actions taken by leaders and decision-makers will help you identify where improvement is required and what unfair behaviors are taking place. Here are a few tips for identifying and responding to bias within the organization.

*Identifying and Recognizing Bias During Recruiting*

When a decision is made to start a hiring process for a new candidate, a job description will likely be written and posted in several places to attract the best talent. People fail to see that the way these are written might lead to some people not applying because of the language used. Employers must be mindful of stereotypes and specific words that can intimidate an individual from applying. This could mean using inclusive language, refraining from mentioning education or social background—categorizing candidates in general.

Think about it: If you place candidates on separate piles because of one characteristic, you could be unintentionally biased. This could mean making a pile for men and one for women; one for Ivy League students and one for those who are not, and so on. Once you're able to identify this behavior, avoiding it will become much easier. Leave aside your judgment and personal experiences and look at the information with no opinion.

This process can also be applied to the ever-growing use of video interviews. As recruiters, we tend to take in everything that involves using a camera in the hiring process—the background noises, the place where the person is, and if there is any interference—none of which determine if they can carry out the required tasks for the job. If we refrain from forming an opinion on the other based on what their homes seem to be like, for example, we are promoting an equal opportunity and leaving bias aside.

For in-person interviews, this will include judging the person based on their clothes, appearance, and behavior. Are you giving this more importance than you should? You could be focusing on more than the individual's physical characteristics in their resume, skills, and abilities. You could be focusing on an accent, which will not impact how well they perform their job. If you focus on anything rather than their experience and what the individual can bring to your organization, you are likely to be biased.

Therefore, the question is, *how can I effectively respond to bias and remove it from my company and its processes to create a more diverse environment?* There are several options, and, as I said in the beginning, it will involve having the stakeholders' full cooperation. You've already taken the first step: identifying it.

## Strategies for Responding to Bias

In order to respond to bias, we need to look at it from two angles. The first is for those conducting the recruiting process, and the second is for the actions taken within the company. While the first will help you bring more diversity and inclusion to the organization, the second aims to reduce bias others might have toward these new employees and their future activities.

To start, let's look at the hiring process. The initial step is to standardize the process to have equal comparison parameters. This means asking all the candidates the same questions in the same order—especially those that will identify skills that will directly impact their performance when carrying out their responsibilities. The opposite of this would allow an interview to be guided based on the candidate's answers and personalize the process. Another helpful tactic is to apply standardized tests for them to answer that will help identify their characteristics. These should be carried out before the personal interview to enable a filter to be set and can include forms related to management skill set, mathematical abilities, or writing an essay. All will depend on the type of position you are searching to hire for.

Addressing the second example might be a little more complicated since bias is something that we all have and can be deeply rooted within a company. To avoid bias, the HR department should conduct training and awareness sessions for the current employees and listen to what they have to say. Carrying out surveys and other methods of addressing employees can be an important barometer to determine what needs to be adjusted and taken care of. Assessing your company's demographics and employee ratings will give you a holistic view of how the company is performing and the proceeding steps you should take to make DEI more present in the organization.

## TECHNIQUES FOR MODIFYING BEHAVIOR, POLICIES, AND PRACTICES

Once the company has decided to change and implement these within the organization, it is time to think about ways to make this happen. Although it will not be easy to change corporate culture–or even people's behavior, in that case–there are a few techniques that will help you with this task. Most involve communication, so be prepared to invest heavily in this department to get your ideas through to others.

Most of your efforts should be directed toward training and creating awareness. There are several ways this can be carried out: Online training with specifically developed and targeted programs, formal sessions within a classroom, as well as hosting lectures with specialized speakers. Another positive way to conduct sensitivity training in the organization includes educating employees through role-play exercises, in which they will perform as several characters according to the targeted needs.

When you immerse your staff in situations where they can go through the experience that the others might undergo, it will make it easier for them to understand one's experience. It will also enable them to assess their feelings and analyze their biases and how they could judge others. This practice tends to have a positive outcome since it will provide them with a safe space to ask questions, practice action, identify behaviors, and receive feedback.

This feedback, however, should not only be a part of the training process. Employees should be encouraged to discuss DEI issues within the organization. They must be provided the chance to voice their thoughts and concerns regarding the company's policies and attitudes, especially where they identify problems and space for improvement. This will enable the company leadership to have a perspective different from theirs and allow them to modify any ongoing misbehavior.

Once you have conducted training and created awareness, you will probably need to reinforce your intentions through internal communication. When company leaders spread the message through official organization channels, this shows employees a certain level of commitment. Expressing and demonstrating the expected behavior within the company and how everyone's participation is essential in changing and modifying the *status quo* will be one of the most critical attitudes throughout the transformation phase. Decision-makers and stakeholders will be responsible for putting into practice what is expected to be done and their conformity to the new policies and procedures.

These new policies and procedures will be one of the last parts of your program. The company must establish and adhere to its new rules regarding hiring formats, giving promotions, and dismissing employees. A standard will need to be set as a guidebook on how specific processes should occur. This will initially be important, especially to help employees who have worked in the company for some time and might need help assimilating the new rules. As time goes on, this will become more natural, and less orientation will be required. Once this happens, you will see that DEI is already a part of your company culture.

## CREATING A MORE EQUITABLE WORKPLACE ENVIRONMENT

Once you have determined a strategy for implementing a DEI framework within your organization, it is time to create a more equitable workplace. This means that you will need to start enhancing diversity awareness and understanding through the methods you have chosen with the company's leadership. To begin the process, create an action plan with all the steps you tend to take. This plan should have established dates and deadlines for specific actions. Set milestones to determine specific points within your plan that will bring a significant change or project implementation. The action plan should take as stipulated, and you might want to create several actions that work simultaneously.

In most cases, groups can work in collaboratively in different areas of the company to implement DEI practices. For example, while one team might be working on writing the new procedures that will be put in place, another could be searching for people who can conduct training sessions. The work of both groups would be simultaneous but would end together by having the employees' point of view on new procedures after they have been trained.

This process will be ongoing and subject to changes as you learn, and because of this, it will need constant monitoring and evaluation. To monitor the effectiveness of your plan, think about key performance indicators (KPIs) to measure the success of the DEI initiatives you carry out. Monitor these numbers and conduct periodic reviews of the results to see if there has been a change. If you need to, use technology to amplify the reach of your program to reduce bias. In addition to sharing the results of the changes with the company, create a safe space for individuals to speak up. You might want to do this through an anonymous suggestion and complaint channel, creating ERGs, and providing mentoring sessions for employees with people who are not their direct supervisors.

Being mentored by someone other than the one you report to might benefit all parties. The main reason is that people tend to not speak their minds truthfully if questioned by a person with direct power over their jobs. When this happens, the management's unconscious bias can be a barrier to creating an equitable environment in the workplace. Recognizing and acting on it will be the first step toward eliminating it. Work to modify behavior, policies, and practices to ensure everyone is given equal access to resources and opportunities.

You might now think that company-wise, implementing a DEI initiative will be complex and costly. You are not entirely wrong. A budget will need to be allocated to the initiative, and awareness training can be expensive, especially if carried out continuously. However, have you ever wondered how much forgoing DEI costs your company? Most likely not, but as you will see in the next chapter, it might be more than you expected.

# HOW MUCH IS IT COSTING YOUR COMPANY NOT TO HAVE A DEI STRATEGY?

According to research from Bersin (2019), companies with diverse teams see 2.3 times as much cash flow per employee over three years. The study was conducted across over 450 global companies in three continents, all of which had more than $750 million in revenues. Furthermore, Gompers and Kovvali (2018) state that having diverse ethnicity in organizations led to increased success in investment rates, with a percentage of 32.2 compared to a 26.4% rate of less-diverse companies. Additionally, the IPO acquisition rate was 11.5% lower for a non-diverse organization compared to one with DEI initiatives.

But these numbers are just the tip of the iceberg. They are just what can be seen on the surface and what can be concluded by analyzing public market numbers. The impact of not having a DEI strategy affects a company much more than what can be seen in news outlets. Organizations that do not have a DEI strategy tend to lose more–more opportunities, talent, investments, and market share. In this chapter, I will show you the direct ramifications corporations suffer when they do not implement a DEI culture. Let's take a look at how DEI is much more than allocating budget or increasing earnings–it is about action.

## COSTS OF NOT HAVING A DEI STRATEGY

If you think about the following questions, what makes a company? Who does having a DEI strategy favor? What makes an organization grow? The answer is easy and direct: people. You might have realized there is a common denominator here that will determine the success of your company and its performance.

As leaders become more conscious of the need to implement DEI strategies in the workplace, the idea is supported by widespread social pressure from minority groups. People are not just looking for a paycheck at the end of the day, anymore. As more time is spent performing work-related tasks within the office walls, employees want to feel like they belong and are respected for what they are. Once people start feeling like they are not represented within a corporation, the natural course of action is to leave and look for an environment where their needs will be met.

While many companies claim that they have an inclusive policy, management's perspective can be widely different than that of workers. In a 2018 study by Accenture, 98% of 1,700 leaders claimed that they considered their company inclusive, while only 80% of their employees felt that they were represented (Ward, 2020). The result? These American companies missed out on saving $1.05 trillion in expenses due to lower turnover and increased productivity. This was the impact the unrepresented 20% had in the general corporate economy, which could have seen a 33% increase in profits otherwise.

Apart from the high turnover generated by the lack of diversity, companies that do not have an inclusive approach fail to attract talent in the market. Individuals who do not feel represented by an organization are less likely to apply for a position within it. In addition, the loss includes missing out on opportunities to innovate, creating new products, and engaging with a diversified public. On the other hand, companies that invest in a diverse workforce see an increase in productivity, engagement, and overall satisfaction in the workplace.

But what differentiates companies that invest in DEI and achieve results from others that also dedicate a budget to the initiative but continue to experience employee, customer, and market dissatisfaction? There is only one word I can think of, and that is supported by several specialists and studies: commitment. Many leaders believe that just dedicating a budget to diversity and not actively acting upon it will generate a positive result. Others are not patient enough to see the results and, at the first lack of significant results, start cutting the budget and placing it on other initiatives. The truth is that these individuals were never really engaged and committed to making a change, and people see it. And what is worse; the incorrect application of a DEI framework within an organization can be more damaging than not trying at all.

Companies that fail because of a lack of investment and engagement in implementing a diverse and inclusive approach, face severe reputational problems, especially at a time when everything is on social media. Today, people can publicly voice their concerns, impressions, and the lack of an effective policy, possibly damaging the organization's image in the market and affecting its future revenue. In addition, it may be perceived as a place that does not care about its employees, but rather more focused on increasing company profits, regardless of the cost, including deceiving others with supposed policies.

But what about companies that act upon the established strategy? What is the positive outcome for them? While it might seem that just the opposite of what you have just read would be enough of a positive effect, there are a few others that I can think of. These include increasing employee morale and company revenues, as we will see in this chapter's next section.

## THE ROI OF INVESTING IN A DEI STRATEGY

If seeing the negative impacts on your company is not enough to convince you to implement a DEI strategy, maybe some benefits will make you feel otherwise. Although we will take a more detailed look in Chapter 5, I would like you to quickly glance at the ROI of investing in DEI.

When you create a culture of inclusion, you are first and foremost leading to better business outcomes. In a study conducted by Harvard University, it was found that there was a direct relationship between diversity and innovation after examining over 1,700 companies in more than ten countries across the globe (Lorenzo & Reeves, 2018). The study found that these companies "had both 19% points higher innovation revenues and 9% points higher EBIT margins, on average."

The main reason is that these companies improve employee engagement, retention, and performance, leading to better performance. In another study, Lunaria Solutions (2019) claimed, "regardless of the size of your company, we are consistently seeing that companies that invest into DEI see a revenue increase by up to 41%."

Two significant impacts include improved brand reputation as well as customer loyalty, increasing their competitive advantage. Furthermore, a positive brand image by employees translates to good reviews on social media and among their social circles, which is likely to attract and retain diverse talent. When others see that a specific company respects and includes minorities, they tend to become a place where people want to work in and collaborate. This will bring innovation and creativity, enhancing employee engagement simply because they are trusted for their talent and no other reason.

As you can see, when you invest in a DEI strategy, your company will reap beneficial results—financial, cultural, and talent-wise. At the same time, those companies not thinking about this can be susceptible to economic losses that reflect not retaining talent and losing good professionals to other organizations. This will be especially true if the organization only has a superficial DEI undertaking and employees feel it does not practice what it preaches. In this case, the damages can be even more significant.

Some companies that have efficiently implemented a DEI strategy have already begun reaping its benefits. In the next chapter, we will see case studies of how companies innovate in this area and how decisions impact their businesses. You will observe that DEI is reshaping how America sees its employees.

# 4

# DIVERSITY IN THE WORKPLACE — CORPORATE AMERICA'S OVERDUE FACELIFT

> *When we're talking about diversity, it's not a box to check. It is a reality that should be deeply felt and held and valued by all of us.*
>
> — AVA DUVERNAY

Saying that diversity has become critical to companies in America is not enough if there are no examples of success to illustrate that. In this chapter, we will look at five companies that have successfully implemented a DEI strategy in their culture and the positive impact it had on their employees. Although I have selected only a few to illustrate its application, the initiatives continue to grow and make a difference even as you read this book. More companies are rethinking their strategies and approach, looking to achieve success with their DEI initiatives.

## THE ANSIRA CASE

Gale (2020) told us the story of a successful DEI strategy in the company, Ansira, where its leaders were able to identify their biases and make a change to the company. She mentioned that the company had no diversity approach until a new employee detailed the impact diversity training had on the team in their former company. He took it upon himself to search for a consulting company that specialized in diversity to carry out training sessions for the company's management and leadership—three sessions were required to remove the impression that placing a DEI strategy was more than just the "charity case" that most people think it is.

Once the training sessions were finished, the participants could identify their biases, especially in their speech when referring to those who are part of minority groups. It made them realize that while addressing a white male, for example, they used positive words regarding their achievement; when describing a black female as important to the team, their introduction was more based on a description of what they do. Despite neither being negative, this showed that sometimes, our unconscious bias gets in the way of business. Leaders and managers could reflect on their attitudes and communication based on the bias they recognized in their behavior.

According to employees heard by the author, the training sessions were considered a success, with employees still talking about it sometime after it occurred. Sources say they can see the changes in how the business is conducted and how people or minorities are treated within the workplace. Another positive impact included improving the communication between employees regarding diversity and equality, as leaders recognized their bias and volunteers offered to help take a more active role in DEI initiatives.

The company is currently holding DEI training sessions for all employees and is establishing KPIs to measure the progress of these initiatives. It is also performing assessments and establishing ERGs to identify and diminish problems related to a need for more inclusive activities.

## AUTISM AT WORK BY SAP

At SAP, the organization has committed to a company culture which includes hiring individuals who are neurodiverse, more specifically, those with autism. According to Woo (2019), the program began in 2013 and aimed at diminishing the 80% unemployment rate of individuals within the spectrum. As a result of the program, leaders have been trained to manage neurodiverse individuals and adjust their practices to make these employees feel more comfortable in the workplace. Numbers from the program showed that it was, and continues to be, a success. SAP has a more than 90% talent retention rate within the spectrum because of the support system it provides to employees.

## TRANSFOCUS AT MOZILLA

In an effort to support employees undergoing gender transitioning, Mozilla implemented guidelines and policies for these individuals. They worked with a company dedicated to the subject, looking to make the transition less stressful for its staff. According to the company, given that many people spend more time at work than at home, it is essential that they are provided a space where they feel safe and can express themselves. This includes being respected for who they are and teaching others how to be inclusive. This means encouraging others to use the new social names and pronouns of the individual who has transitioned and facilitated changing their information within the company's systems.

The company also assigned mentors and health managers to help through their processes and new benefits. In the report by Robertson (2019), employee testimony shows that the program has worked and that those who underwent transition feel as if they are in a safe place. The company also invests in training and gender awareness sessions open to all employees. They have specialized ERGs that work with those who have doubts and questions. According to the report, this has positively impacted the company, with employee engagement rates drastically rising.

## FEMALE LEADERS AT VERIZON

In another example of inclusive practices, telecom giant Verizon established a program to place women in positions of power in the company. According to Kinloch (2020), one of the main reasons for this was that they identified that having women occupying senior management roles could help increase its profits by 30%. This included adjusting to their needs and demands, and including women who would make a difference in the science, math, technology, and engineering fields—historically male-dominated fields.

The company implemented the program throughout the organization, enabling hundreds of its employees to apply for management positions and opening opportunities for promotion. The program received recognition and awards from industry bodies for its initiative. Inside the organization, women felt more empowered, and the *climate* in the company improved with these professionals being able to significantly contribute to the workforce.

According to the program speaker, Melanie Miller, cited in the report by Kinloch (2020),

> [Women] show up in all shapes and sizes, colors, hair colors, haircuts, women with fuchsia pink hair, women dressed in men's suits, in high heels, in flats, all ages, gay and straight, able-bodied and disabled. The irony is that the organization is making an investment in them, and it is they who will ultimately give back to the company (p. 5).

## BE YOURSELF AT JOHNSON & JOHNSON

Last but not least, I want to illustrate what is happening within the pharmaceutical giant Johnson & Johnson. The company has a global inclusion and diversity policy that is headed by a Global Diversity and

Inclusion team, which has a vision and several missions. Among the individuals in the program are veterans, LGBTQIAP+, people of different ethnicities, and women. The company has placed inclusion within its guidelines, and several ERG groups were formed to support the initiative. According to an internal survey carried out by the company, 90% of the company's employees felt that its leaders supported and respected diversity in the workplace (Johnson & Johnson, 2021).

The company applies its DEI strategy within its walls and through suppliers and partners, making this a general policy. This includes training and teaching employees about diversity, recognizing talent, and promoting opportunities for offices to implement new strategies and programs. Johnson & Johnson states that they hold leaders accountable for their actions, including hiring a diverse workforce. According to their DEI report, in 2021, 48% of women in management positions and 33.9% of management positions in the United States were held by employees with diverse characteristics, such as ethnicity and race.

IN OTHER WORDS

As you can see, diversity in the workplace is becoming increasingly important in corporate America. Companies that enforce the decision to apply DEI practices are experiencing long-term growth and success. Although not all initiatives are the same nor do they focus on the same groups, there has been an effort by large companies to be more inclusive. In the next chapter, I will discuss more numbers on how DEI benefits the bottom lines by creating a profitable and market-competitive organization.

# 5

# HOW DEI BENEFITS BOTTOM LINES

A study conducted by McKinsey & Company showed that companies whose executive teams are more gender-diverse have a 25% chance of being more profitable than those in the lower quartile (Dixon-Fyle et al., 2020). This is only one of the advantages of having a diverse workplace. However, to ensure that the initiative has a positive outcome, companies need to be aware that they need to invest in it—which mainly means putting money into something that will provide a financial benefit in the long run. Let's look at some numbers that should be considered as an incentive to establish a DEI initiative.

## THE FINANCIAL BENEFITS OF DEI

Since the murders of Breonna Taylor and George Floyd in the United States in 2020, American organizations seem to have finally noticed that they need to invest in reducing inequality. As a result of the public protests that were carried out after their deaths, corporations in the United States, more specifically the country's top 50 companies, pledged to invest more money toward racial justice.

To understand where this money went and if the companies stood up to their promise, Jung (2021) investigated if the money was indeed invested. According to the findings, these public companies and their foundations had committed approximately $49.5 billion to address racial inequality. Out of this number, the author claims that almost 90% went to loans or investments that they could later profit from, especially as mortgages, while $4.2 billion was given as grants to Black and Latino students to go to college.

While ensuring these communities have a home by giving them access to mortgages, JPMorgan Chase has provided that these people have better living conditions and grasped an essential share of the previously overlooked market. Not only have they helped with inclusion, they also secured new clients. It was a win-win situation.

Other initiatives include purchasing more services and products from diverse companies and using more black-owned banks and corporations. The policy change and attitude have started making a difference in the market. According to the study conducted by McKinsey and published by Dixon-Fyle et al. (2020),

> Organizations in the top quartile for ethnic/cultural diversity among executives were 36% more likely to achieve above-average profitability. At the other end of the spectrum, companies in the bottom quartile for both gender and ethnic, cultural diversity were 27% less likely to experience profitability above the industry average (p.2).

Unlike a time when companies used to be silent about their diversity and inclusion numbers, companies today take pride in showing that they are trying to change the past. This means that companies such as Google, Apple, and Facebook now use these numbers as an advantage for propelling their stock and image with investors. A Kellogg Insight report (2020) based on a study conducted by scholars has shown that:

> Every additional percentage of women on staff at the time of a company's first announcement was associated with a 0.1 percentage point average increase in stock price. Meaning, all else being equal, if two companies released their diversity figures on the same day, the stock price of a company with 40 percent women would increase by one percentage point more than the stock price of a company with 30 percent women (p.16).

The main reason for these numbers, according to the study, is due to the fact that investors tend to favor companies that have more women in management. Even if the number of women in these markets is still low, there is a tendency that they will continue to grow. This means that bringing diversity to companies, especially for those organizations that act under market scrutiny, could mean a boost in profitability, when compared to industry averages and companies without the same initiative. An example of this was given by Levine (2020), who reported that:

> There is ample evidence that gender diversity drives results. Women are well-situated to know and understand market opportunities. Women control 51% of U.S. wealth (40% globally), and

women either directly make or influence up to 80% of all purchases. No wonder that Bloomberg reports that companies with gender-balanced teams have a higher return on equity (p. 6).

From there, all the company will see are benefits based on the correlation established by over ten studies conducted. But we do not need to go far. Suppose you think about an organization with a positive sentiment of diversity in the market. In that case, you can deduce that it will have increased revenue from new products, especially coming from social media insights. More revenue from sales means more profit and a positive effect on a company's market valuation. To sum it up, we could say that the minimum action an organization takes will create a ripple effect that will continue to generate long-term results. What is better, everything points toward them all being positive.

## THE IMPACT OF DEI ON BUSINESS PERFORMANCE

Knowing that you know the positive impacts of a DEI framework on your company, it is time to prepare a business case to present to management and the organization's stakeholders. To make a compelling business case, you must first identify the business goals and connect them with the benefits of implementing a DEI strategy. This will help you identify the business's priorities and how starting a DEI framework will impact business performance.

There are some questions that the stakeholders will need you to answer that mainly include the *how* and the *why* this initiative is essential. However, the most critical question you will need to answer is *how much?* To be sure that you are giving accurate numbers and information, you will need to evaluate the costs for the program you want to start and how much of a budget would be necessary. Link these numbers to the company ROI and make sure that the data you collect points to achieving higher performance and results.

Presenting accurate data and real-life case applications will be an excellent motivator to have stakeholders invested. Although we will dive deeper into their participation and engagement in the following chapter, I want to take a moment and mention that it is unlikely that you will have success if they are not involved. Implementing a DEI strategy needs to have the participation and acceptance form the company's major players to be successful. In this case, I suggest speaking to people, conducting surveys, and trying to identify the pain points and areas of improvement.

After you have identified the company's needs and identified how a DEI strategy can fit in, showing the decision-makers what they would benefit from implementing a DEI strategy is the next step. This can include comparing existing costs to savings that would result and the profits that could be earned. To illustrate your point, focus on numbers such as turnover and talent that has decided to go elsewhere because of the lack of diversity. You can link these numbers directly to show the potential benefits of establishing the program. My suggestion here would be to focus heavily on numbers, returns, and profits, highlighting the financial benefits that the strategy would bring.

Remember, that for a plan to be effective, there is no need to start big. You can create minor procedures and changes to see the project's evolution. Set KPIs and measurement systems to compare the past with the present and the changes that can be seen. Join efforts with other departments, such as marketing and other human resources areas, to see the impact this change has had in the company on the outside and the inside. See how the new strategy links with the company vision and mission and adjust it accordingly. Establish goals for the program and plan the steps you will take toward implementation.

To ensure that the program is seen and that everyone is involved, setting benchmarks and milestones for each action you take might be interesting. You will need to monitor these goals and likely adjust them as you go. If needed, keep an eye on employee behavior and hire an external consultancy company or a specialist to assess and evaluate your program. People with more experience tend to have different views on certain aspects of a DEI initiative and present out-of-the-box solutions to problems we have yet to identify.

This includes aiding you in dealing with and being prepared to face pushback from some people. Some employees might think this is just another initiative or it is just being done on the surface. One of the negative impacts tends to happen when you establish quotas and targets—some employees might feel as if they are being left behind to the detriment of a minority. If this is the case, you will need to focus on training and explaining the initiative to everyone in the company since they need to see the larger picture and how this will positively impact the business.

## CREATING A SUSTAINABLE COMPETITIVE ADVANTAGE THROUGH DEI INITIATIVES

Creating a culture of inclusion is a must today, especially if companies want to remain competitive. By starting a DEI program in your organization, you will be able to establish an advantage over competitors who do not. Most companies that include DEI within their strategy see an increase in their indicators—one example can be observed in the stock market. Investors tend to choose to invest in one company over another due to the DEI initiatives they observe. This is even more true if the investments you want to attract come from millennials.

Recent research claims that 74% of this group prefers companies that apply diverse practices (Peatman, 2021). One of the main reasons for this is that diverse teams open doors in communities that could not be reached before. When you have minorities represented by the company's staff, it is more likely to attract other members from these groups and, consequently, diverse talent. I want to give a quick example regarding this.

Suppose you are part of a minority group browsing through LinkedIn. You see a picture of a management board composed of white, middle-aged men in suits and another composed of men and women of different ages and skin colors. Both of them have job openings and are hiring. Which one would you rather choose to apply to? Which company would give you more chances to grow in your career as a person from a minority group? Understanding the need for diversity to attract talent and investments includes putting yourself in the other's position and understanding what they see from the outside and how the market perceives your company.

Additionally, if innovation and reaching new markets is what your management is looking for, there is an interesting statistic: companies with diverse management teams tend to have a 19% higher revenue based on innovation (Peatman, 2021). It seems unlikely that a less diverse team can understand the demand for a specific product within a minority group. When you attract diverse individuals to work in your company, you also open up the opportunity to get to know new cultures and develop products for unmet needs.

To give you another example, I want you to go back to 2018. During that year, Faber-Castell decided to try a new strategy in the Brazilian market. You might not know this, but Brazil is racially and ethnically diverse, with white people as the predominant group. Seeing the need to create a more inclusive approach with customers in the company, this year, they decided to incorporate six additional colors into their coloring pencil line representing the country's more diverse skin tone. The boxes that contained its products were also updated to represent a more inclusive population.

Can you imagine the impact that this decision by Faber-Castell had on its consumers? Although the company did not provide numbers regarding the outcomes of this strategy, all I can say is that if the financial result was not positive, the moral one was. I could keep on going with examples—the market has several I could provide you with. However, I think that by now, you have seen the advantages of implementing a DEI initiative in the workplace. More importantly, you have seen that these have a tangible result in the business. Results of DEI implementation can be made; they are not subjective but directly impact organizational performance.

It is important to remember that while they create a competitive advantage, most of the results are not immediate. You need to have patience and think about it in the long term. This includes maintaining your stakeholders engaged in the matter, even if they do not see immediate results. This process takes time, effort, study, and engagement. The first step will be to build the framework in itself. If you are wondering where your starting point will be and how to begin, read the next chapter to find out.

# 6

# BUILDING A DEI FRAMEWORK

❝ *Inclusivity means not 'just we're allowed to be there,' but we are valued. I've always said: smart teams will do amazing things, but truly diverse teams will do impossible things.*

— CLAUDIA BRIND-WOODY

As I briefly mentioned in the previous chapter, we will look at how we can build an efficient, and equally effective, DEI framework. To do this, you will need to engage all the stakeholders in your company and ensure they are on board with the program and, most importantly, committed to it. First, list all the people interested and affected by your new framework. Identify them and try to see what points resonate the most with them. While you might have a leader focusing on financials, another might be worried about the company's turnover.

When you give the management team the numbers that will excite them, there is a better chance that your outcome will be positive. You will also have them engaged and interested in your project. The C-Suite, composed of the CEO, CTO, CIO, etc., aligned with the senior leadership, will be the propellers of the initiative and help diffuse it throughout the organization. If there is no commitment from their side, there is less chance of success.

On the other hand, you need to keep in mind that you must also engage the employees, not only the company's management. To do this, you should focus on using their emotions to guarantee that they are invested in the initiative. While the administration will likely use a more intellectual and rational approach to the subject, you will see that it makes a difference when you get passion from those who make up the workforce. The main reason for this is because they can probably relate to one or another minority group—ethnic, racial, gender, religious, or other.

To measure the impact and acceptance of your new framework, it is best to start with a small survey on the employee impression regarding DEI in the company. You will better understand what, when, and where to attack first, based on what the stakeholders say. Once again, I want to remind you that starting small and progressing might be the best idea—this is a marathon, not a sprint, so take it easy! There will be no benefit if you decide to implement everything at once!

Before the survey, it would be interesting to specify situations that explain unconscious bias and attitudes generated from it. You can use role play, presentations, lectures, and other resources to precisely exemplify what you are trying to change. This will enable the company's professionals to understand where they are doing wrong and create a better image of what needs to change. After this, conduct the survey and listen to what they say.

Based on the survey results, you will create a plan, but, more importantly, you will create DEI accountability systems. When speaking about stakeholders, you cannot take their initiative and participation for granted. This means keeping them excited about the changes that you are making after they have decided to support you. Some companies find this is the major problem when implementing a DEI strategy—everyone seems on board with the programs and changes until stakeholders do not start seeing immediate and effective results. There are several ways to measure the success of your new project and guarantee employee engagement. The first and most important of them is what I will talk about: employee resource groups, or ERGs, as they are commonly known.

## INITIATING AND LEADING EMPLOYEE RESOURCE GROUPS

When you think about implementing a DEI, the first thing that should come to mind is to start an ERG. This means you will create a group led by employees focused on diversity and inclusion throughout the company. The company should formally support this initiative, and employees should be grouped based on common characteristics such as race, ethnicity, socioeconomic status, gender, religion, lifestyle, or interest. "The groups exist to provide support and help in personal or career development and to create a safe space where employees can bring their whole selves to the table" (Hastwell, 2020).

### *Creating an ERG Structure and Purpose*

When you want to start an ERG, the first thing you should do is set an objective: What is the purpose of this group? What is it trying to achieve? What employees or groups of people are you trying to reach or attract? One of the end objectives of the ERG is to promote employee awareness and improve the work environment. By giving the employees a safe place to express themselves, you create an environment which is conducive to them sharing their experiences and bringing added value to the company.

It might be helpful to start a diversity council in the company with representatives that will support and aid the ERGs in their operation. Hastwell describes an ERG as being both top-down and bottom-up—this means that these groups should receive input and support from management and that the employees also need to play their part in ensuring that the groups are relevant. You might consider bringing in someone from outside HR to lead or co-lead the group. Some companies pay employees to perform this role, while others make it a voluntary position. You should ensure that the chosen person is a natural leader and that their voice will be heard and respected at all levels of the corporation.

Another extremely relevant thing is to give employees time to work on the ERGs during their work hours. As this tends to be a voluntary initiative, it is unlikely that people will feel attracted to it if they have to work beyond their schedule. It will also be essential that the financial and material needs of the group be met—to start a program, raise money for a cause, or prepare an event. If the company is invested, a part of its budget will be directed toward supporting these groups to make their work more efficient and relevant.

When you adopt supportive measures, it is more likely that employees will become engaged in the process. However, management support is also essential on a moral level. They must support the initiative and allow their team members to participate. The positive outcome of connecting employees of different areas and expanding their network should be made relevant as much as giving them availability to support members during difficult times. "Once people feel connected and protected by the organization they work for, they're significantly more likely to participate in the majority culture and work toward the success of the organization" (MentorcliQ, 2022).

Once you have the members and the structure of the ERG in place, it is time to take one last significant step in the process: formalize its existence and prepare to announce its purpose to all employees in the company. Here, you will need to establish a mission and a vision for the group and set objective goals that they are trying to achieve. Its activities will need to be prioritized, and the actions they want to take will be planned according to the organizational agenda. Finally, establish how the ERG will earn the money it needs to support its initiatives, as well as a motto. After all this has been done, it is official! You have started your first ERG in the company. Now, it is time to put it to work.

## BUILDING A DIVERSIFIED INTERNAL PIPELINE FOR PEOPLE MANAGERS AND LEADERSHIP POSITIONS

As the company and your commitment to establishing an effective DEI program in your company grows, there will come a time when important structural decisions will need to be made. You will need to start thinking about creating an internal pipeline for people, managers, and leaders. Having an inclusive approach also means that you will need to provide employees with the opportunity to grow within the company's management and develop themselves.

Whether you will only focus on key roles by building specific structured paths for them to make it a more widespread initiative, will depend on the guidelines you are given. In either case, you must be aware that you will need to educate the existing managers to infuse the

DEI values into the leadership culture and have them promote these programs among the other employees.

My suggestion here would be to start small, prioritizing certain roles that have more impact on the organization. This can be done by analyzing department structure, performance, and reach. The company numbers you will be provided with will give you a better idea of the most significant and critical roles. Putting this into practice will also require the HR department's essential participation and its recruiters' participation.

You will first need to identify the entry-level position that will lead to the leadership role and determine what steps need to be taken to reach it. Based on this, recruiters will search the market for people with diverse characteristics to fill the position. In this case, the recruiters need to know what to look for, which will require training and specialization so their biases do not interfere with the process. One of the examples where this initiative is successfully taking place is Netflix. According to McLaren (2020),

> Netflix's inclusion recruitment team works with around 200 recruiters throughout the organization to help them develop this skill set. That way, no matter what team is hiring, someone will be on hand to offer recommendations and ensure

best practices are being followed—resulting in a more inclusive, equitable approach (p. 6).

To attract talent from diverse groups, my suggestion would be to review the job descriptions you have and the way you publicize new openings. When recruiters speak to potential candidates, they should consider the potential shown rather than previous work credentials. One of the reasons this is important is that, as part of a minority group, they may have never been given a fair chance to show their true abilities due to unconscious bias.

Another important part of the process will be opening the candidacy for new positions to employees already within the company. You might be able to identify individuals suffering from bias before the initiative, which shows they can grow and develop in the organization based on their reputation and performance. For this reason, you might need to review the performance assessment process and speak to their leader to better understand this individual's characteristics and profile. Promoting open vacancies in the company so that people can find their right fit will help attract potential hidden talent within the organization.

Finally, once you have filled the positions and established a career path for these individuals, it is time to start investing in them. This could mean having an outside speaker address the potential future leaders or have them participate in off-premises leadership training. Another initiative that could be set is to offer coaching sessions and mentoring to these people. Throughout the process, it will be essential to monitor their growth and progress to ensure that the investment is being made in the right place.

To ensure the success of your initiative, you need to focus on collecting viewpoints from multiple people in the organization, as well as listening and observing. Start with the ERG groups and their members. Ensure they are supported by the leadership and the C-suite. Provide these employees with a safe place and show them how much their time dedicated to the group is important.

Once these ERGs have been established, and are fully functional, you can use their input to modify job descriptions and make them more attractive to diverse talent. This talent will be chosen to build the new management pipeline in the organization. Once you create a diversified pipeline for people managers and leadership positions, you will see that implementing the DEI framework will become easier.

Now that you know how and where to start, we can move on to the next phase of your project. For this, you will need to answer a very important question: What is my company's culture regarding DEI? Understanding the present status and improvement points within this scope will be essential. If you don't know where to start, do not worry, I will guide you through the next steps in the following chapter.

# TAKING THE PULSE OF YOUR COMPANY'S CULTURE

> *Determine what behaviors and beliefs you value as a company, and have everyone live true to them. These behaviors and beliefs should be so essential to your core, that you don't even think of it as culture.*
>
> — BRITTANY FORSYTH, VP OF HUMAN RELATIONS, SHOPIFY

Once you have established your goals and objectives for your DEI initiative, you will need to understand if these have been accomplished or are on their way to being so. Assessing the current state of your DEI framework will be important to see if some improvements and adjustments need to be made. To gather this information, there is no better way than obtaining data and feedback on the various metrics and KPIs you established at the commencement of the program.

"Different metrics focused on DEI are used for different purposes, but all are valuable and can be used to identify risk areas, prioritize initiatives, set targets, and other program goals, assign accountability, and measure the impact of initiatives" (Survey Monkey, n.d.). In addition, you must identify if what is being achieved aligns with the company's objectives and the business plan you initially established. Let's look at a few indicators you can analyze to measure your success.

The first thing you should analyze refers to **money**. You should determine whether any budget is allocated to DEI initiatives and if they are being used to amplify and support the program. In addition to this, this is an interesting time to look over the payroll and award bonuses for your organization's employees. Analyze if there is a difference in pay among people who have the same role but are from different groups. Since the principle of equal pay should be an essential factor in your DEI plan, looking at potential disparities will help you understand where you need to improve.

Next, you will need to look at **employee retention** and **turnover rate**. These are both important metrics because they could mean employees are uncomfortable working for the company. When thinking about retention, you will need to consider the quantity of voluntary and involuntary departures and compare them to the employee satisfaction surveys. Here, the main target of your evaluation will be people who belong to diverse groups—a higher retention of these talents means that the result of your program is positive.

While looking at retention and turnover is important, you will use the metrics you obtain to determine the **demographics across your organization's groups and levels**. This means, identifying if employees of diverse groups are being hired and promoted, if they perform relevant tasks, and if they feel comfortable carrying out their tasks. Compare these numbers to those obtained before the program started. In addition, you will want to determine the percentages of diverse individuals within each area and their perception of the program. Ask questions such as: Do they think they are being well represented? Do they believe their opinion matters? Do they feel relevant to the company?

To make your analysis even more significant, you will need to review the number of **incident reports** referring to people from diverse groups. However, equally as important as the number of reports are if the employees feel comfortable reporting issues to HR. The numbers should decline as your program gains momentum, but this should result from increased awareness rather than individuals feeling intimidated to report any problems. Analyzing this metric might take more effort since employees might fear retaliation if they report inappropriate behavior.

Listening to the employees and taking note of their **feedback** will be essential—especially when coming from individuals from diverse groups. Their opinion regarding the initiatives and the changes that have been made will enable you to understand if you are on the right path. Their opinion will be the most important and will also show you the places that need improvement or stronger action. Listen to their thoughts and engage the ERG groups to provide a report on their members' opinions regarding the change in the organization. You might find that while you are right on the spot with part of the program, others need reinforcement to produce better results.

The final suggestion I want to make regarding KPI monitoring is establishing the **participation rate in DEI training programs and events**. This will show whether employees change the company culture and environment. When you measure participation in training, you must ensure that these sessions lead to change in the organization, especially regarding management views (Hall, 2022). This means analyzing the number of participants per session, the number of representatives from management levels, training program offers, assessments of their impact on the workplace, and the rating given by the attendees. Another efficient way to measure this is by analyzing how what was learned continuously impacts the workplace and how it is being reinforced within the company.

MEASURING ENGAGEMENT

When you set out to measure employees' engagement with the DEI initiative, you should first consider conducting a survey. Surveys are efficient and practical ways to measure satisfaction, allowing you to establish indicators and translate them into easy-to-understand numbers. When preparing the questions for the survey, keep in mind the company's critical areas. Doing this will make it easier to determine what should be asked. Critical areas that should be included in the questionnaire are:

- leadership
- recruiting/screening process

- hiring committees
- pay practices
- microaggressions
- complaint management
- training procedures

You can target these areas by asking closed-ended questions that directly target the new actions for the program. When you attribute a scale of satisfaction from 1-10, for example, it will enable you to establish a quantitative index. In addition, it might be interesting to get a few employee testimonials to present to management. While you might expect most of them to be positive, be prepared to have a few negative comments that need to be addressed, urgently. All the feedback you receive will point out important indicators regarding the success of the DEI implementation.

When you evaluate diversity in the workplace, it is important that people feel safe to express their opinions and concerns. For this reason, I suggest conducting an anonymous survey, where employees should not be forced to give up their names while answering. This might make them more comfortable expressing ideas and what they feel. The questions you apply on this survey should have similar, if not identical, questions to the one you carried out before establishing the DEI program. By doing this, you will be able to compare results and see if there is an improvement in the workplace regarding diversity and inclusion.

## IDENTIFYING AREAS FOR IMPROVEMENT

After assessing employee engagement, it is time to analyze the results. Based on the answers, you can determine the next steps that need to be taken. These include, but are not limited to:

- reviewing and revising current policies.
- understanding if and what sort of targeted training is needed.
- determining the need to create accountability systems.
- identifying gaps that were not addressed by the current program.
- establishing potential areas of concern.

Since the questionnaire applied was separated into potential concern areas, it will be easier to establish what to target first. You should make a list of all the problems that were identified and see what the best courses of action are. If you struggle to find a solution aligned with the business goals, you might need to look outside the organization.

Comparing your program to others in the market might be an excellent solution to the problems you identify. You can use benchmarking and contact other professionals in the diversity area to see where you are going wrong and what can be improved. You can also use solutions others have applied and adapt them to your organization's needs.

Once you have measured and identified all the issues with your DEI program, you will need to take action. It is now time to create an action plan and establish the next steps needed to improve the program's performance within your organization.

## CREATING ACTION PLANS TO DRIVE CHANGE AND IMPROVE PERFORMANCE

Creating an action plan following the plan's first assessment will help you to establish accountability, adherence, and responsibility to the program. The action plan should be determined according to the metrics that have proven to be lower than expected and that are not achieving the goals and objectives you have set within the established timeframe. Assigning specific tasks to key individuals will help change these numbers, and thus, the importance of having measurable objectives.

Since the main idea of your program is to drive change and impact organizational culture, it is imperative to ensure that these goals are still achieved even as time goes by. This might mean better communicating better your efforts and the changes that have been implemented, showing the benefits that the program has brought to the workplace, and leadership commitment in numbers, such as recruiting for diversity.

Building a DEI program is the responsibility of all members of the company, and the way leadership deals with it will impact the results. Ensure that the goals for your action plan are SMART: specific, measurable, achievable, realistic, and time-bound. Further along in Chapter 9, we will explore actions that can be taken to include in training and initiatives and how to make these work in your organization.

For now, keep in mind that one of the most important things you will do after your DEI program has been implemented is to evaluate its performance. This means measuring employee engagement and evaluating policies to identify if any improvements are needed. If they are, you will need to create an action plan to drive change and improve performance, and one of the keys to success is what we will talk about now: looking for influencers within the company that will help you garner a buy-in.

# 8

# FINDING CHAMPIONS

Although DEI initiatives may seem daunting, organizations can cultivate the necessary support to make real change. With the right champions in place, any organization can create an environment of inclusion and acceptance. When I speak about champions, I mean people who will be truly invested in the initiative and will work to ensure that it is successful. These can be executives, managers, or employees that you feel have leadership characteristics or whose opinions are usually heard by others.

## THE ROLE OF DEI CHAMPIONS

Your DEI champions will be those people that you count on to make the program successful. While ensuring that all levels of the organization are involved in the process, having management buy-in will be essential to make the program work. Without the company's top leaders, your program will be very unlikely to succeed. *But how will I attract management to invest in my program?* That is a very good question—and one of the answers can be summarized in one word: data.

When you are seeking to attract individuals to participate and engage with the program, you will need to convince them that this is not only the correct *moral* attitude to have, but also an initiative that will benefit the company. You can gather evidence demonstrating DEI programs' business value and the cost of not paying attention to diversification initiatives. When looking for information to reference from, you can search the following sources:

- numbers and examples I have provided you with in this book
- HR journals that show numbers on DEI
- news articles that exemplify how other companies are developing their own programs
- corporate websites for companies that already have an implemented program

- statistics and research papers that explain and demonstrate the positive effects of DEI programs in organizations
- information obtained from social media related to the subject
- notes from training sessions you have attended and data provided by special consultancy firms.

Once you present the players you have in mind with all the relevant data, it will be easier to have them onboard the program. Ensure that you have targeted the right leaders within the company and that they understand and are attracted to the business case you built. Use your knowledge to change the DEI narrative from something that needs to be done because of social pressure, to one that states that it will bring the company benefits and added value.

Banjoko (n.d.) suggests "helping the CEO to see how the issue affects those people from the relevant minority that are already working in the business (however few their number)." This is also related to any of the other C-suite members within your company. If they feel like a DEI initiative will benefit the organization's overall result, then you can be almost sure that they will accept the role of being your champion.

As the HR leader, you will also have a role in stirring your champion toward supporting the program; you will need to ensure that they have all the necessary support to make the program go forward. Facilitating their work and helping them prepare will be significant parts of the task to ensure that the priorities you have set move in the direction you want them to. Having an influential leader or leaders participate will strengthen your initiative and make it more relevant to everyone else.

## LEADING EMPLOYEE RESOURCE GROUPS TO ADVANCE DEI INITIATIVES

While a champion will be needed to help your initiative take off, another type of leader you will need to identify within the company's employees are ERG leaders. These can, but don't have to, be from management, but they must be part of the group they represent. According to Seen at Work Team (2022),

> The most common ERGs include associations for women, employees of a particular race or ethnicity, and LGBTQIA+ employees. But ERGs are also emerging to represent people with disabilities, veterans, working parents, genera-

tional groups, and other shared dimensions of identity and experience (p. 3)

You will first need to establish what groups you want to represent and identify their potential partners and advocates. Since minorities tend to naturally associate with each other, this might make it easier for you to identify those who are interested. You might want to look within these individuals to see if anyone is already exhibiting model behavior and leadership qualities. However, be aware of the potential tokenization of these groups based on their appearance, belief, or other characteristics.

To attract employees to your ERGs, create meaningful incentives for those passionate about DEI. This includes giving them time during their shift to work on the group, ensuring that they have access to members of the C-suite for discussions, funding to carry out projects, and validating job descriptions for new positions. These ERGs need access, and ideally members, of all parts of the business since they will directly contribute to the organization. According to the Seen at Work Team (2022),

> Only 20-60% of companies leverage ERGs in various aspects of business development, compared to over 90% that rely on ERGs for

internal community-building. This is a missed opportunity, as ERGs can connect with new customer segments, contribute innovative revenue-generating ideas, and provide insight to improve business outcomes (p.6).

Motivate ERG members or group leaders to become mentors and show the benefits of having their group represented in the company. Show them that they can be a motivator for change, that they can impact the organization. When aligned with the DEI champions you have identified, you will establish an effective structure upon which to set your program. Leaders will enable you to develop the recruitment process to identify and develop potential champions and engage stakeholders, creating systems for tracking progress and providing meaningful rewards for employees.

*But what will be included in the guidelines of the program? What should I establish? What should be considered, and when should each action take place?* These are all common and valid questions when you start thinking about your program. To help clear your doubts, in the next chapter, I will address these issues in the next chapter and propose solutions that you could apply to your business.

# WHAT TO INCLUDE IN YOUR DEI TRAINING AND INITIATIVES

Companies who have committed to implementing a DEI framework within their culture often find it hard to maintain the initiative. In an article published by Corrigan (2022), it is reported that only 34% of companies claim they can actually afford to support their DEI programs. This is in spite of the fact that 81% of the interviewees believe that the DEI initiatives are important to the company. The main problem may be exactly in the last statistic mentioned by the author: out of all the surveyed companies, only 49% claim to have a strategic plan in place for DEI.

As you know by now, preparing and establishing what steps you will take are a key part of the process—they will enable you to determine when to implement and what actions need to be taken. Therefore, the lack of a plan seems to be the main issue that connects these companies. What is even worse, they are not applying the main key to identifying progress or stagnation: surveys. "Only 40% of organizations are conducting DEI-specific surveys, research shows. That's disappointing because to make progress on representation, companies need to collect more data on the demographics and experience of their workforce" (Corrigan, 2022).

The number is supported by the source of information, the Culture Amp (2022), who states that only 27% of the employees surveyed believe their companies know how to survey DEI initiatives. Therefore, it is not only a question of measuring but also how these KPIs and achievements are measured. Another alarming number brought by the publication is that while 95% of the employees believe that the organizational policies are in place to motivate DEI, 58% of them believe they are not enforced by the company.

But what makes a DEI initiative successful? What should the program consist of to ensure employees are happy and encouraged? It is not one thing but rather a set of actions and initiatives that will make applying, understanding, and conveying the project to all employees a success. Read on to learn more about tips and suggestions that will propel your program, make it

## DESIGNING DEI TRAINING PROGRAMS

The first point in your strategy should be to train the company's employees. This does not mean hiring formats or content used for several companies. Here, you need to remember that with DEI, there is no "one size fits all" and that any initiative should be tailored to the organization's needs. Since this might require some study from the company and dedicated time to understand the underlying issues, it will likely have an elevated cost. Therefore, be sure that you have the resources and the budget to carry out these sessions.

While the cost might not be attractive to the company's C-suite, once again, this is why you have your champion—they should be an active player in convincing the management that this approach is needed and that funds need to be allocated to the program. The program you select should address unconscious bias, prejudice, taking action, and the benefits of setting a DEI initiative. The awareness sessions also need to come from a credible company—using the wrong language, examples, or situations to exemplify problems may create a stereotype that will not be helpful, thus excluding minorities even more.

Another issue you need to remember is that these sessions must be ongoing and happen periodically. Therefore, it will be helpful to create a timeline for training initiatives and adapt them as you measure employee engagement and the results of the actions taken. These periodic sessions should be a part of the goals and objectives you are establishing and the employee participation rate in them. However, beware of having employees just "complete" the course, "Simply breezing through course content doesn't cut it any longer. To deliver a shift in mindsets, overcome biases, and drive lasting behavior change, L&D teams must look beyond just DEI training course completion" (Pandey, 2021).

When speaking about goals and objectives, ensure the person or company that you hired to speak has their speech aligned with company values, mission, and the program's objectives. Within their program, they should include addressing and confronting bias in the workplace and how to avoid segregating these groups. Also, as a part of the training and awareness, you could, for example, have an ERG representing a religious group, teach employees about their culture, beliefs, and traditions. Building awareness is one of the main instruments you can use to train the professionals in your company.

Incorporating these nuances that are specific to your company will help create a friendlier environment and avoid specific types of conflicts. You need to understand your audience and discover their perspectives regarding these subjects.

Lastly, to ensure that training has been successful, you must establish checkpoints and evaluation processes. While setting an overall goal for the program will be useful, you also need to determine the specific outcomes of each training and ensure that the subject approach will "stick" to the participants' minds. By ensuring that the training and awareness sessions have had the desired effect, you will then be able to establish a culture of acceptance and respect within company walls.

## INCULCATING A CULTURE OF ACCEPTANCE AND RESPECT

Although it might seem hard to change what people think and have them accept and modify their bias, there are a few techniques you can apply to make the process easier. The initial point is to create a system that encourages open dialogue—at all levels of the company. A great place to start is with leadership's approach, where they show that they are willing to change and make a difference. People in the organization's top management should demonstrate that acceptance and inclusion are skills that can be learned and implemented within the company if everyone participates. Leaders will need to be the role model for your program, and once other members of the organization see that they have bought the idea, they will follow the cue.

It is also important for you to create safe areas where people can express their thoughts. This can be through mentorship, ERGs, or any other solution that your organization is willing to accept. In this space, employees should feel they are free to talk about any problems they might be having regarding being part of a minority and voicing their opinions. Providing what is called "psychological safety" will make people feel safer and give them a place to be vulnerable. "When you have psychological safety, people will feel empowered to speak up and speak out to truly take action against bias" (Young, n.d.).

Creating these groups is only a part of the solution. You should also work toward developing different programs that aim to create awareness among the employees. The size of each of them will depend on the budget you have allocated to DEI, but it can be as simple as celebrating a Heritage Day to a full week of events dedicated to diversity. Motivate your employees to participate in them by offering rewards and recognition to those who participate in the initiatives. Your imagination should have no limit. You can also use the opportunity to listen to employees and ask them what they would like to learn, discover, or gain from these programs.

Ensure that all the initiatives you prepare point back to overall company core values. You can use this as an opportunity to reinforce the company's mission and strategy with employees and show how diversity and inclusion are directly related to achieving success. If people believe in their organization's corporate culture, it is likely they will be more than happy to participate in initiatives that add value to it.

Use your position as the HR leader to communicate with employees and facilitate moderating conversations. You should use all tools you have for communication to create awareness and share initiatives. In the next chapter of this book, I will give you several options for communicating your DEI initiative, projects, and achievements within the company.

## USING TECHNOLOGY TO ENHANCE LEARNING EXPERIENCES

When creating a DEI program, technology can be your ally—use it to obtain the most of your employees' learning experience. The first part of the process is identifying the right tools that will best adapt to your work environment. Suppose that all employees in the company have a computer at their workstation. If this is the case, using e-learning could be an efficient tool to train employees, especially if you decide to use a learning management system (LMS) tool.

By providing employees with digital training tools, you can extrapolate the training experience so that each one can carry out the sessions at their earliest convenience. You will also be able to develop effective learning materials with company-wide reach with modern software. By creating a fun experience where employees can create their own avatars and immerse themselves in the presented situations, you can also create different trainers and sessions based on your needs.

Another positive point of using LMS is that you can monitor and assess employee results in the tests that need to be taken after each session. This will create a new KPI that will enable you to see if there are any specific themes that need more investment or attention.

Providing all employees with equal access to information makes it easier to identify where you need to improve your communication or the awareness process.

Suppose there is a specific minority group that has no representatives in your company. Using the LMT will enable you to expose employees to their reality nevertheless, since you will be using an online tool, thus making the process more culturally inclusive. The same can be said for those who do not have vast representation in the organization. "If employees don't see themselves represented or their unique needs addressed within training materials, they're less likely to participate. This cultural bias can make employees feel like they don't belong and less inclined to stay engaged in their work" (Cross, 2022).

Although online training is one great example of a cost-saving and wide-reach technique, remember that each training program will need to be adapted to your company's reality. In a factory, for example, it is unlikely that employees dealing with the machines have access to a computer unless there is a laboratory they can use. Therefore, it will be up to you to identify the right tools and effective learning material to use in your organization.

Independent of the tool you select to carry out training, ensure to include resources, measurable objectives and goals, a timeline for implementation, and an evaluation process. Once you notice that the initiative has a positive outcome, you'll know that you're on the right track to seeing more results. Remember that inculcating a culture of acceptance and respect relies on creating systems to encourage open dialogue and programs that foster understanding.

# 10

## TIME TO SPREAD THE WORD

> *Diversity really means becoming complete as human beings — all of us. We learn from each other. If you're missing on that stage, we learn less. We all need to be on that stage.*
>
> — JUAN FELIPE HERRERA

Now that you have your DEI framework ready, you need to start making people aware that it exists—after all, why would you have an initiative if people do not know about it? Communicating its existence to all stakeholders will reinforce the organization's commitment to it. After all, it is being made public, and, therefore, will help to establish accountability and responsibility.

Your communication will need to reach people inside and outside the organization—this will help attract talent and new clients, for example. As you will see in this chapter, while some initiatives will need financial investment, most of them are simple and do not require any budget. Read on to learn about some of the options you have to communicate your DEI framework to stakeholders.

## EIGHT WAYS TO PROMOTE AND COMMUNICATE YOUR DEI FRAMEWORK

Communicating your DEI framework will require more than typing a memo and sending it to all employees saying, "Hey! We now have a DEI framework! Click on the link to learn more!" Using the previous example, albeit simple, will not create any engagement from company employees and might even seem dismissive or that it is not being given the appropriate attention.

Although there are several better ways to do this, you should take into consideration the use of inclusive language, the openness to ask questions and discuss ideas, and, most importantly, a strategy to amplify what you want to say. As you will see in the examples that I have outlined for you, many of these actions do not require money since you will be using channels that already belong to the company. However, you might want to invest in a specialist to double-check the content of the information and the tone of the message you want to send.

Choosing the appropriate communication format will help you to efficiently convey the message and specify if an answer is necessary. Depending on the chosen channel, you can include a call to action and establish a connection with the community. When developing a communique, remember to focus on the needs of those who you are writing about and evaluate possible outcomes for what has been said.

Once this has all been considered, it is time to choose one, if not all, method of communicating your DEI framework to the world.

*Use Internal Communications*

Internal communication channels will be the most efficient way to spread the word within the organization. You can use the company's intranet, message boards, email, and town halls to share what is being done. You can start off by having a message written by the CEO, informing the teams about the new initiative and their view on the matter. Having a message from top management will bring credibility and assurance to employees since they will be ascertaining their buy-in, one of the requisites you have already seen is necessary for the program to thrive. Another alternative is to use the company's internal newsletter to communicate the program's changes and the results. In a nutshell, be creative! Use the available tools to create engagement and share your actions and their results.

**Develop Engaging Content**

When thinking about the material you will use to spread the word on your DEI framework, you need to create engaging content that will attract the stakeholder's attention. Create visuals, videos, and other interactive elements to share on social media platforms that tell the story of the organization's commitment to DEI initiatives. Developing content that users can interact with will go beyond the need to just read text, which tends to have higher engagement rates. Additionally, using pictures and other visual material will help others relate to your objective and will be easier to remember, while making an impact.

**Leverage Social Media**

Most people today communicate through social media. In the same way that your organization can receive negative reviews because of the lack of diversity, you can use it to your advantage to show what you are doing differently. To create effective campaigns, engage employees, stakeholders, and the public in conversations about DEI initiatives through social media channels. Use LinkedIn to communicate what has been done and to show your program's results. Interview employees from diverse backgrounds and publish the outcomes of said interviews. Use inclusive language to ensure that all audiences are reached. Giving your company more social media exposure will immediately attract the attention of others outside the company and entice them to learn more about what you are doing.

### *Hold Events*

Holding events is one of the most efficient ways to create awareness concerning your DEI initiative. You can use the opportunity to host workshops, seminars, or other events to discuss DEI topics and foster learning among employees and stakeholders. Depending on your budget, you can also host weeklong events that will approach different subjects in diversity and inclusion during employee working hours. You can, for example, have a theater company present a play on the inclusion theme, carry out game sessions related to the theme, and propose challenges that will earn employee points if they conclude "missions." In addition to this, you can carry out an *international week* where people from different backgrounds talk and teach their culture to others, including cultural presentations. Think creatively and listen to opinions from different members of the community to ensure that everyone has a great time and that they assimilate the material.

**Give Public Speeches and Interviews**

Since your DEI initiative is something that you want to make public, engaging the C-suite and other leadership members to speak to the public about its impacts on the company may prove to be an efficient tactic. Make executive team members available for public speeches and interviews to discuss your organization's DEI practices. This includes sending press releases to media channels that can learn more about the program. Enlist your marketing team to help you communicate with news outlets and create material that you can use. This can include professionally-made video and written interviews, creating a podcast for your company, or speaking at public events. Any opportunity leadership members have to spread the word on what is being done within the company will prove to be fruitful. Here, you will need to take one precaution: Ensure that these people are coached and know what they have to say. Otherwise, they could place the whole program in jeopardy.

## Celebrate Achievements

A good way to communicate the success of the DEI initiative is to celebrate company milestones and achievements. Take time to recognize employee contributions to the organization's DEI program and successes in achieving DEI goals. People tend to be honored by these shows of appreciation and post them on social media. This will create indirect engagement from outsiders without the company's interference. At the same time, when you reach an objective that is part of the global strategy, do not hesitate to publish and celebrate these publicly. This will show your engagement in the process and commitment to making and maintaining change.

## Showcase Partnerships and Awards

You can probably think about entities that hold "best place to work" surveys and awards. These tend to be carried out by consultancy companies and media outlets that interview employees and come up with a scale to measure their happiness in the workplace. To ensure that your company is moving in the right direction, volunteer to participate in these initiatives. If you happen to win an award or enter the raking, this will be positive free publicity for your company to work with. You can also volunteer to undergo audits and appraisals from outside companies to evaluate your program's application. Highlighting partnerships and awards related to the organization's commitment to DEI and sharing them on social media channels, will bring more attention of diverse talent.

**Connect With Outside Organizations**

As you might have seen by now, communicating your DEI efforts is something that needs to be carried out, both internally and externally of the company. Other than just using outside companies to benchmark initiatives or ask for help when implementing your own, you can use them to highlight your program. Look for ways to collaborate with other organizations on DEI initiatives, as well as opportunities to support each other's efforts. This could mean creating a work group with HR members from companies within the same industry to meet periodically in order to share and discuss ideas. You can search for individuals who already work with DEI through social media and connect with them.

There are many ways for you to promote DEI initiatives—it is up to you to decide what best fits the company culture and, of course, your budget. Remember that these techniques should be used to communicate effectively with employees, stakeholders, and the public about DEI efforts. Furthermore, remember that when you spread awareness of these initiatives, you are ensuring others that DEI is a priority across all levels of the organization, especially with the company management.

# 11

# HOW TO CHANGE MINDS FROM THE GROUND LEVEL TO THE C-SUITE

A successful DEI program can not only increase employee morale and productivity but also help to attract a larger and more talented pool of job applicants. However, getting people to change their minds or address their biases might be challenging, especially when you need to resonate with everyone at all levels of the organizational chart. The main reason for this is that people have different backgrounds, experiences, and cultures, which means that each one will digest information in their own way.

In this chapter, I will provide tips and best practices for engaging executives, managers, and employees who transform the organization into a diversity-focused company.

## ENGAGING MANAGERS AND THE C-SUITE IN DEI INITIATIVES

Creating a culture of acceptance at all management levels will be a determining factor for success. Having the managers and the C-Suite understand that implementing a DEI framework will bring financial and cultural benefits to the company are two of the many advantages that they can be presented with. When you mention a new approach to the subject, you will need to demonstrate that the program will be effective and that only benefits will be the end-result.

However, only *accepting* the program and not participating in it will not do the trick in most cases. The organization's top and middle leadership should lead by example for implementing DEI practices, including addressing systemic issues at the root level. One of the steps you might need to take is to invest in training programs for these individuals and motivate them to participate and engage in DEI initiatives to show their commitment. In essence, if they agree to buy your idea, they will need to be guaranteed that this will not only be "another HR program" that will be managed and taken care of by the department—they need to commit to all levels of its application.

Managers should be the first to adopt DEI practices by addressing them in the recruiting process. They should be aware of their bias and conduct hiring processes that consider diversity and inclusion. One of the actions they can use for this is to conduct an anonymous review of resumes, where the names, gender, age, and any other relevant characteristics will be removed from the file. This will enable leaders to judge and select the best candidate according to their talent and experience.

Another practice leaders can apply, with the help of the HR department, is to enable employees to provide anonymous feedback regarding company policies and attitudes. Initially, they might feel that this can generate disruptive opinions and unfavorable feedback, it will also show where the organization needs to improve and provide support to the teams. Management from all levels needs to be ready to address their biases and behavior regarding members of diverse groups—including the manner of speech, approach to promotions and salary increments, and task division in the workplace.

According to a report published by Dillon and Bourke (2016), an inclusive leader has six defining characteristics. These include:

- **Curiosity** to learn new subjects and listen to different ideas to experience growth.
- **Cultural intelligence** to identify that people come from different backgrounds and cultures and that because of life experiences, the same event can be perceived differently depending on where you are.
- **Collaboration** to guarantee that employees work together as a team to achieve the objectives and goals as well as to believe that when people from diverse backgrounds work together, the final result will be positive.
- **Commitment** to see the process through to the end and maintain their stand even when things get difficult or engagement decreases.
- **Courage** to admit their biases and assume they are not perfect, which can lead to personal risks with company stakeholders.
- **Cognizance** to admit their biases are their point of weakness.

Once leaders in your company can relate to these six issues, it will be easier to have them commit to the DEI initiative. However, getting them on board will only be part of the solution. Next, you will need to find a way to ensure that employees are engaged and of the belief that corporate culture will change and that they will only have to gain from it. One of the best ways to conduct this process is to empower them to lead the change you want to see.

## EMPOWERING EMPLOYEES TO LEAD CHANGE

Employees are tired—of organizations proposing change and not seeing them through. "Employees have endured months of rapid and constant organizational and business change and are battling concerns about the economy, job security, their health, and the health of their loved ones" (Baker, 2020). Because of this, what companies are experiencing can only be described as resistance to accepting and incorporating changes into their work environment. Most of them think, *if my managers are not applying for the change, why should I?* Or maybe *Why should I be the one to make an effort to change when no one else does?* There is also the *Again? Another change?*

These are just some of the most common reactions HR departments face when they propose an organizational and culture change. This phenomenon is called **change fatigue,** and it "manifests in negative reactions such as burnout, frustration or apathy—and results in lower employee engagement and productivity" (Baker, 2020). The changes that impact employees don't need to be big, the smallest structural change might already see resistance from those who have had enough.

Based on this current scenario that most companies are facing, you might be asking yourself *If I cannot have the employees change their minds, how will I motivate them to lead change?* That is, in fact, one of the hardest challenges that your DEI program might face as you try to implement it. The lack of motivation comes from many places, including the lack of belief that things will change or that things are just being done to make the company look good. To turn this around, you will need to show employees that an effort is being made by all levels of the company and that they will be the ones responsible for making change happen.

Here are a few tools you can use to motivate employees to participate and lead change:

- Show employees that having a DEI initiative will promote career development and growth opportunities.
- Demonstrate that adopting a DEI culture in the company will create an environment for open dialogue and feedback between all company levels.
- Ensure that all management levels will be accountable and responsible for their actions,

which will be measured through KPIs and ongoing evaluation processes.
- Encourage management and leaders' participation in discussions about DEI and have them as role models for the actions you want to adopt.
- Give employees a sense of purpose and direction concerning the DEI framework.
- Provide support and funding for ERG groups and initiatives they might want to carry out.
- Offer benefits such as time off or other types of gratification for people who participate and engage in DEI initiatives, such as ERG groups.
- Give employees time to work on DEI projects during the workday, so they feel motivated to participate.
- Allow employees to take the lead in subjects that are the most important to them and with which they can closely relate.
- Make them feel as if they belong to the team and that their input is necessary and valuable to make things work.
- Invest in technologies, events, training sessions, communication, and supporting material that will show the organization's commitment to the cause and that will enable everyone to participate.

- Encourage employees to have a sense of ownership in DEI initiatives by listening to them and the feedback they provide regarding the steps taken during implementation.

In addition to these points, you might want to avoid promoting too many changes at once. If employees are presented with a "big bang" of changes, it will be harder for them to assimilate everything all at once. This will also show employees that you care about how the changes affect them and how it might impact their job. People, in general, tend to be resistant to radical changes, so going easy is the way to go.

Nevertheless, you must remember that implementing change will likely be disruptive and cause some internal conflict. For this reason, it is important to secure the participation of management, and even employees, with moral leadership among their peers. Once you have this step concluded, you will see that the DEI initiative you want to implement will have a bigger impact on the rest of the company. Guaranteeing the participation of influential members will give your program strength and credibility.

To spread acceptance, use different strategies and techniques for each group you want to reach. For example, the language and indicators you might use with C-Suite might not be the same that you use with entry-level employees. Each group will need a different approach and strategy that ensures there will be progress and accountability throughout the program.

Finally, all company members will need to see progress and change to reinforce participation and commitment. Seeing a shift in company culture and experiencing the presence of individuals from diverse groups will help them see that the program is effective. For this reason, tracking and reporting your progress should be a significant part of your action plan, which we will learn more about in the following chapter.

## "ARE WE THERE YET?" — TRACKING YOUR PROGRESS

Studies show that companies who invest in DEI initiatives have a 36% higher chance of outperforming their peers (Dixon-Fyle et al., 2020). Considering that most of these companies are committed to making change and are open about their results to employees and the market, this gives them an even larger advantage. You should know that just applying a DEI program is not enough—not by far. As the result of an interview with Paulette Alviti, CPO of Mondelez, Cohen (2022) states that "Mondelez discloses certain DEI metrics, like annual compensation for women in senior leadership, and she said this increases transparency for its employees."

Doing this will allow employees to keep track of what is being done and the evolution of the change being carried out. Although I have already given you some insight in the previous chapters on monitoring and measuring these goals, there is much more you need to know. Because of this, in this chapter, I will give you more details on how to set measurable goals, how you can use data to create DEI insights, and ensure that there is accountability for the results obtained by the organization.

## SETTING MEASURABLE GOALS

When you set the goals and objectives for your program, the first thing you should ensure is that you have obtained input from employees at all levels of the organization. You should encourage the participation of individuals from all departments, especially if they belong to a minority. Once this is done, you will be able to establish a few metrics that will allow you to keep track of your progress.

These metrics are different from the goal you have set. Mendes (2022), describes the difference between goals and metrics the following way:

> Metrics are relative and flexible. Two organizations with similar goals might employ different metrics or interpret the same metrics in contrasting ways. Metrics, like KPIs, should help

leaders make informed decisions and provide insight into how well the company is or isn't achieving its DEI goals. Goals tend to be fixed and absolute, as these represent the desired outcomes and objectives you are trying to achieve (p.4).

Here are nine suggestions of indicators you can measure to verify the program's efficiency:

- *What is the number of diverse employees in my company?*

This metric will enable you to identify if there has been any progress in hiring diverse individuals to compose your company's teams. Even if you see that more diverse talent is being hired, you need to compare this number to the total quantity of employees the organization has. This metric will be based on a percentage that compares the **number of individuals from the diverse groups** to the **total number of employees in the company**. Using this approach, you will be able to identify which groups are underrepresented and what areas of the company need more diverse talent.

- *How much diverse talent is being attracted and hired by my organization?*

When you evaluate the organization's hiring practice, you will need to follow three different numbers: the **number of diverse candidates attracted to each job posting, the diversity of the candidates that are interviewed**, and finally, **how many of these are hired**. Suppose you are attracting many diverse talents to each open position, but when you analyze the hiring numbers, there is still no change. This may mean that you might need to provide training for the managers so they can analyze their unconscious biases. Alternatively, you use a diverse hiring panel and anonymous resume reviews to minimize bias-oriented decisions.

- *What is my company's retention rate for certain groups of employees?*

Suppose your company has been facing a high turnover or that members of a diverse group seem not to stay. You will need to understand why they may not feel comfortable in the work environment provided. To understand these numbers, you will need to compare **the number of employees from a diverse group leaving the company, the total turnover number**, and the **number of employees in the company**. If you identify that the turnover points to more members of a certain group leaving, this could mean you need to adjust your DEI program. Based on this, you will need to understand why they left. One of the alternatives will be to implement an exit questionnaire that will enable you to identify potential problems that led to their departure.

- *How many individuals from diverse groups occupy a leadership position?*

Diversity is not only about having people from minority groups part of the entry-level workforce. You need to have people in leadership positions as well. You can calculate this number by comparing **the number of individuals from diverse groups in management** with **the total number of managers** or the **percentage of diverse leaders in the company** compared to the **total number of employees in the organization**.

- *How many of our services or products are provided by companies with diverse approaches?*

When we mention DEI, you need to consider from whom your company obtains its products or who provides services. This means studying the organization's **suppliers** to understand if they also have a diverse approach. You could also analyze if they are owned and managed by individuals from diverse groups and what their inclusion policies are. This could be a big step toward changing the business ecosystem since companies belonging to minority groups tend to be less favored for providing services.

- *Is there equal pay between employees from two groups that perform the same tasks?*

When we consider inclusion and equity, this applies first and foremost to having equal working conditions for employees from all groups. One of the metrics you can study is whether **managers and employees who perform the same tasks receive equal pay**, regardless of their group. This means that if a man and a woman, for example, perform the same tasks and have the same position, their pay should be equal.

- *How many incident reports have we had?*

Although employees might initially feel a little intimidated to report any misconduct that comes from others, especially if they are part of management, you will need to keep an **incident channel** open to listen to any complaints they might have. While having a high number of reports is not good, not having any can also indicate that employees don't feel safe to report any problems they might be facing. Monitor these incident numbers and see where additional training is needed to reinforce DEI points.

- *What is employee participation in ERGs?*

As you know by now, having an ERG will be essential to ensure that your DEI initiative works. One of the metrics you can monitor is the **number of employees participating in ERGs** compared to the **total number of workers that belong to a specific diversity group**. If you identify that the percentage of diverse employees participating in this group is low, you might need to understand why this is happening and structure changes. Getting to the root cause of the problem will enable you to fix any issues and engage more employees toward participating.

- *What are the general employee satisfaction levels?*

The last metric I want to suggest is a broad one—it refers to the satisfaction rates employees feel in the company. Based on this approach, you can measure everything from **how comfortable they feel being part of a diverse group, if they feel the DEI initiative is**

**effective, if they have seen change in the company, and if they believe if the initiative is producing results.** You can measure employee happiness levels and engagement.

These are only some of the indicators you can use to measure if your initiative is successful. While there are many more you can apply, it will depend on the company's objectives and goals to determine the most relevant ones. Each one of these metrics will require a different approach and a unique measurement method. Once you have this data, it is time to decide what you will do with it. This means creating an action plan based on what you have identified to improve the program's numbers and performance.

## USING DATA TO CREATE ACTIONABLE INSIGHTS

Once you have the results of your KPIs, you will need to analyze the data to create actionable insights and an action plan to fix any problems you identify. You should use data analysis tools to conduct effective decision-making and establish the priorities of what will be 'attacked' first. If you have added open-ended questions to obtain some qualitative information, place all the answers on a sheet where you can read them all. In the previous example, I have already provided you with some alternatives on how to solve these issues, although they are not the only ones—your approach will depend on the organization's guidelines and management decisions.

One of the advantages of placing all the data into one tool that will generate the analysis for you is that it will enable easy global analysis of the program. In addition to this, it will make it easier to make conclusions and to present the company leadership with fast and analyzable data. When you present the information, my suggestion is that you bring the numbers you identified and a solution you have designed. This will save a lot of time and discussion and facilitate decision-making. To this, you can add other indicators, such as the allocated budget to initiatives and some statements made by employees that you feel are important to address.

Some of the examples of what can be included in your action plan include providing more budget, having leadership participate more, changing hiring practices, holding more training sessions, and even hiring an external consultancy to help. These are all valid proposals that will be taken into consideration and are more likely to happen if you have the numbers to support them.

Last but not least, you need to reinforce accountability for the results. This means that people need to be held accountable for the presented results. If a manager has a less-diverse team of employees, they need to be coached and trained to address any possible bias that keeps them from hiring diverse individuals. If the company is seeing a high turnover of employees from diverse groups, you might need to strengthen awareness sessions throughout the whole company. If you identify that individuals belonging to minority groups are not being equally paid to same-level employees, it is time to revise the HR policies and obtain support from the C-Suite to ensure that this does not happen.

## ENSURING ACCOUNTABILITY FOR RESULTS

To ensure accountability for the actions that are taken, you will need to create transparent communication channels throughout the company. This means reporting your numbers and results to everyone in the company aware of what is happening. Once these numbers have been pushed and used to evaluate progress, it will be easier to pinpoint those responsible for each area of performance.

To name one example, managers should be directly involved in establishing the goals and must also work to make them become reality. This approach should range from top management and the C-Suite to the lower and middle-management levels. Their goals for the year and the objectives for which they will be evaluated should include their adoption of DEI measures and adherence to the new policy. If you want to see the program become effective, linking their bonuses, for example, to the results they achieve can be one way to go.

Even though this is one effective measure, you need to balance it with providing them with the correct tools to act accordingly. You cannot request that managers act differently from what they are used to if they are not coached and trained appropriately. Providing feedback mechanisms and instructions for them to dial back on their unconscious bias and promote change will be essential. "To make fair and inclusive decisions, company leaders need comprehensive, accurate, and bias-free information about the employees in their workforce" (McNamara, 2022).

Since company leadership will be responsible at the end of the day for ensuring the success of the program, it will be necessary to present them with KPI results and data based on the information you have tracked. This information will enable you to identify areas of improvement and create actionable insights, ensuring accountability for results. "Actions to address lagging indicators (representation, retention rates, etc.) can deliver short-term results, but analyzing trends by utilizing year-over-year results will give an indication of sustainability" (McNamara, 2022).

Once you have established measurable goals, you can determine which events require more participation from a specific department. The communication will become more transparent, and you will find it more successful in tracking progress. This progress should lead to a change in company culture and, eventually, to a successful result in the program's implementation.

## CELEBRATING SUCCESS

According to a survey from Achievers (2018), 44% of employees change jobs because they haven't received enough recognition. This being said, you have probably been in a situation where the employee was leaving and reported they did not feel appreciated or perhaps you've felt the same way before. Sometimes, employees are not looking for money—recognition can come in many ways, and it is up to the company's HR department, and each area leader, to determine when and why each individual should be recognized.

Recognition is a part of our being—we look for it from our parents, our friends, our significant other, our teachers, mentors, and in the workplace, from our management. When there is a lack of recognition, employees tend to feel that the workplace is not so great and that there is nothing to look forward to. This makes production, engagement, and several other indicators fall short. Why would it be different when speaking of a DEI program? Well, it is not.

## RECOGNIZING ACHIEVEMENTS

When you want an initiative to work, all the steps we have already discussed will prove to be effective. However, if you want to *maintain* motivation, recognizing employees is one of the most important ways to do it. With this in mind, leaders and HR should think about ways to recognize the organization's progress regarding DEI initiatives, including rewarding employees for their efforts in making it happen. Although you might think that this is an annual bonus-related issue, it goes beyond this. "Plenty of managers choose not to make it [rewarding] a priority, either because they're too busy themselves or because they simply don't understand why it's so vital to a thriving workplace" (Craig, 2017).

If your objective is to retain talent and reduce turnover, recognizing employees is one way to do it. One of the main reasons to invest in recognition is that it will cost less for the organization to show they appreciate the employee's efforts than it will to hire and train a new employee. "The cost of recruiting and training new employees can be significant, so retaining your current workforce is vital to keeping your company financially healthy" (Garrett, 2022).

Here are five other indicators that might be important concerning recognition programs provided by Wickham (2022).

- Voluntary turnover is 31% lower.
- Employees have a 28.6% less frustration level with the organization.
- 52.5% of employees want to be recognized by management.
- 41% of employees say they want to be recognized by their coworkers.
- Investing at least 1% of your budget into recognition programs will bring engagement results and workplace satisfaction up to 85%.

Recognition programs also tend to attract talent, which is mainly what you are looking for, creating a strong group of employees that will help improve results. Therefore, think about recognition as one of the paths that will lead the organization to achieve its goals and objectives.

If we are speaking about implementing a new program, such as a DEI, acknowledging progress and celebrating the small wins will go a long way. Let's take a look at some of the actions you can carry out to ensure that individuals have the recognition they deserve, that are not directly related to a financial benefit.

## CREATING MEANINGFUL WAYS TO ACKNOWLEDGE PROGRESS

All achievements should be recognized—big or small. After all, reaching a determined objective is a significant step and shows hard work and dedication. However, you need to keep in mind that it needs to be related to a specific event or action. Otherwise, it could prove to be irrelevant. Another point to be considered is that these recognitions need to be timely—there is no real impact in recognizing an employee or a team, months after they achieved the desired result. You should act on it as early as possible: from the celebration to the awarding, to making it public.

Additionally, achievements should be celebrated so that the employees feel gratitude toward them. I used to work for a company where a recognition program was part of the company policy. Managed by the HR department, team leaders could acknowledge their employees by having their pictures taken and posted on the company's communication boards, and a symbolic show of gratitude, such as a pen or a folder with the company name, would be awarded to them. In addition to this, the achievement would be published in the internal newsletter and submitted to the international branch of the group for evaluation. If they were selected, they would be seen by employees globally.

As you can see, this initiative did not require too much investment and used the company's resources. Another thing that should be noted was that the achievement was recognized *publicly*, where the results would be declared to everyone. This is the first aspect you need to consider when recognizing. Whether you will host an event or a ceremony to celebrate the success or create a recognition platform to highlight achievements, there is a solution for every budget.

When you want to create a culture of appreciation and recognition, you need to utilize your creativity and the available tools. Another example of a positive action would be to have the C-Suite and top management recognize an employee's efforts with a personalized message that is made public. Words of incentive can be a huge motivator for those who seek recognition.

Here are a few other ideas you can use to recognize employees:

- bonuses
- financial incentives

- gifts or packages
- days off
- special perks (tickets to shows, voucher for dinner at a nice restaurant)
- gift cards
- something related to a passion they have
- beverages
- better parking space
- high evaluations
- promotions

While the previous list comprises some suggestions, you can set up a committee to establish what you think would be the best approach. Remember, that the recognition process should be something personal that the employee will value. When speaking about diverse groups, this can be something related to their culture, although you will have to, once more, be careful not to stereotype the individual or the minority. Once employees see that the company is adopting this new culture, you will see engagement, participation, and motivation rise, consequently improving their numbers and achieving goal after goal.

## ENCOURAGE EMPLOYEE PARTICIPATION AND ENGAGEMENT

When you create opportunities for employees to be recognized, you also give them the chance to show a little bit of who they are. This will make them feel like they are not "just another number" within the organization. Create opportunities for them to share their success story and what motivated them to work on the initiative. This can be through a social media post, for example, where the company interviews the employee and briefly mentions how important their collaboration to the project was.

If you are considering having a *Diversity and Inclusion Week*, you might want to motivate leaders to participate in the initiatives carried out by employees. What could be better than the company CEO listening and wanting to learn more about your culture and experiences? Enabling this one-on-one exchange will prove to be fruitful because they will feel that someone cares about them and what they do—it shows their voice is being heard and they are being seen. When you show interest in learning more about people, it motivates them and encourages them to bloom and develop.

Feedback can also be a form of recognition. When you tell employees you appreciate the work they have been doing and mention details of what was carried out, they feel as if they are being "seen" and that their work is valuable to the company. If you are speaking about a team, recognizing their efforts will foster a sense of belonging and community, reinforcing the sense of teamwork.

Have management engage and participate in these actions. Once again, the HR department will need to work on providing them with the tools to make it happen if this is something they are not used to. Coach and teach managers what is important, how to show they care, and convince them of the benefits of recognition with numbers. Organizational leadership needs to be aware that celebrating success and recognizing achievements are integral to building momentum toward a more diverse and inclusive workplace culture.

# SIX COMMON MISTAKES LEADERS MAKE WITH DEI INITIATIVES

According to a recent survey conducted by Survey Monkey and reported by Wronski (2021),

> One-third of workers (33%) [in the United States] say their organization is doing "a lot" of work on diversity and inclusion today, and another 37% say they are doing "some" work on DEI issues, while 14% say they're doing "just a little" and 12% say they are doing "none at all." Nearly half of all workers (47%) say their organization's focus on diversity and inclusion has "stayed about the same" over the last year, but a substantial 39% say the topic has become more

of a priority in that time (just 10% say it has become less of a priority) (p.9-10).

When you compare these numbers to some of the previous data that I have shared with you, something will not make sense: If most companies are applying a DEI initiative, how come only 33% of the employees say that there is an effort to implement it within their organizations?

Some of the reasons may include the C-Suite and management not engaging and not taking the program seriously, the lack of communicating goals and achievements, lack of commitment from employees, not being transparent with results and metrics, ineffective strategies, and lack of action plan, to name a few. In this chapter, I will show you the six most-common mistakes made by companies that lead to a failure of the DEI programs or to the employees believing that there is no change in company culture.

## MISTAKE #1: NOT TAKING DEI SERIOUSLY

The first and biggest mistake a company can make is not to take DEI seriously. If there will be no commitment or dedication from all levels of the organization toward the initiative, it is better not to even start it. This can lead to serious reputational problems, as the company will likely publicize that it will put the program in place, and simply abandon it if the results are not seen quickly. GoCo (2022) supports this line of thought and states that:

> The whole purpose of these initiatives is to ensure that team members from all walks of life are equally supported, included, and have equal opportunities within the organization. DEI that's full of empty statements and promises become evident very quickly—your team WILL notice (p.10).

Because results will be important, you will need to set clear goals and metrics to measure the progress of the program. Creating ambiguous objectives or constantly changing them will make the program lack credibility. Once these have been set, the organization as a whole has to work together to make them come true. When these are unclear or there is no guideline to measure the success of the initiative, it will become abstract and difficult to show progress.

Another issue that shows lack of commitment is allocating insufficient resources to DEI efforts. Although the budget may not be as significant as you may wish, you need basic financial resources to make the program run. Doing so will enable it to match desired salaries requested by diverse talent, ensure equal pay among individuals with the same responsibilities, provide resources to ERGs, and provide funds to carry out diversity programs and training sessions.

Last but not least, the focus needs to be on the employees, since they are who will determine the success or the failure of the initiative. If there is diversity fatigue due to the lack of communication, employees will not engage, leading to an unsuccessful program. The importance of employees on all levels cannot be undervalued and needs to be taken seriously. Safe to say that if there is no employee involvement, there is no change, which leads us to the second most common mistake.

## MISTAKE #2: NOT INVOLVING STAKEHOLDERS AND PARTNERS IN PLANNING PROCESS

If you are planning to implement a program in the organization, the first thing you need to do is listen to what stakeholders and partners have to say. You could be missing out on important information when you overlook the importance of having their input or the need to listen to different perspectives. For this reason, stakeholder involvement during the planning process will be detrimental to the success of your program. "The ideal state is for D&I to sit outside of HR and layer over everything the organization does, including things such as clients, marketing and communication, IT, suppliers, and facilities" (Vozza, 2020).

Some companies think that DEI initiatives can be carried out without help or involvement from external companies. This is rarely true. There still are few specialized companies and professionals in the market dedicated to incorporating DEI in organizations. You will likely need their help to make the project move along. This can be as big as developing the whole strategy for your company or as simple as carrying out an assessment to identify improvement points and help you build an action plan.

MISTAKE #3: FAILING TO PRIORITIZE ALL ELEMENTS OF DEI

The initiative's name should say it all: diversity, inclusion, and equity. If you are implementing a DEI program, you should focus on these groups and ensure that you have established actions to prioritize them. This means focusing on the recruitment and retention of diverse talent, prioritizing diversity training and awareness sessions, and addressing unconscious bias in the workplace.

You will need to establish initiatives that will work toward diminishing the gap between the organization's current situation and having a diverse workforce. When you are prioritizing diversity, there should be no "ifs" or "buts." Everyone should be committed to the initiative and make their best effort to apply the program that was set in place.

To this effect, Nguyen (2021) states that,

> A common mistake many organizations make is to expressly focus on the "D" in DEIB. Adopting just this limited view, leadership teams focus on only what's outwardly visible or compositional diversity, so the numeric and proportional representation of different groups within an organization (p.5).

## MISTAKE #4: IGNORING THE IMPORTANCE OF INCLUSION AND INTERSECTIONALITY

You might know by now that having a DEI initiative is more than just hiring and training employees—it should reflect in all aspects of the organization. This means creating an inclusive environment for diverse individuals and groups, as well as ensuring they feel a sense of belonging in the company. Although this does not mean that all actions must be taken at once, it does translate to your initiatives needing to consider all aspects of diversity to create an inclusive environment.

Take, for example, a company that focuses on only one diverse group for its organization. According to Santos (2021), this is more common than not, and can lead to stereotyping and reinforcing bias and diversity fatigue instead of having employees motivated to change. She uses the following example to demonstrate the situation:

> Many companies decide to initiate their DEI efforts by focusing on a single group, like "women." By doing that, they ignore the identities that exist within that group—in the case of women, that of black women, queer women, women with disabilities, etc. That's not only ineffective, but it can also be harmful in the long run (p.5).

To ensure that this does not happen, you need to focus on the metrics, and the data you have gathered that will back up your program. Thinking that an individual can belong to more than one group or that they are intersectional will help you avoid the problem of incorrectly focusing on a specific trait or characteristic.

## MISTAKE #5: INADEQUATE TRAINING AND RESOURCES

Initiatives, programs, and processes need investment. Individuals must be given adequate tools to make their work efficient. This means both access to financial benefits and support through training and awareness sessions. To ensure that a DEI initiative is successful, resources will need to be allocated to the project, depending on the company's capabilities. This does not mean that all investments need to be done at once or that a significant part of the yearly budget should be dedicated to this.

Not at all. It just means that those working to implement DEI should receive a sufficient amount of support to be launched and to be carried out. If the company management is certain of adopting this strategy, they will need to prioritize diversity training and holding events for employees to ensure engagement. This line of thought is supported by Tolbert (2020), who claims the same:

> If leaders are serious about making real change, then diversity managers must be given the tools they need to make an impact, whether it's monetary resources for internal training software or

time with the C-suite to fast-track executive buy-in (p.18).

This means that enough investment needs to be made in comprehensive training regarding DEI topics. It also represents that the organization will provide the necessary tools, technology, and support that will aid in making the program a success. As the saying goes, "if you are going to do it, do it right!"

## MISTAKE #6: LACK OF ACCOUNTABILITY AND FOLLOW-THROUGH

Failing to hold individuals accountable for their actions might prove to be a big deficit in your strategy. This ranges from the lack of follow-through on DEI initiatives and promises, to the lack of taking action when complaints are filed. One of the main reasons this happens is because of the lack of measurable KPIs and metrics in relation to your DEI program. For company leadership to be held accountable for their actions, you need to be able to confront them with the inactivity or underperformance, which will only be justified if you have the data to prove it.

Grannis (2022) makes a point about this when he states that:

> What gets measured gets done. The same can be true for what people are held accountable for also gets done. DEIB programs and initiatives that don't have accountability built into them are less likely to succeed. Changing an organizational culture to be more respectful, value others, and inclusive won't be done overnight. It will require long-term commitment and this means that those involved will need to be held accountable. Managers should be the first priority, and then employees (p.6).

IN OTHER WORDS

When your organization makes the decision to invest in a DEI program, they need to be certain that they will see the process through until it has achieved stability. Most organizations fail in their initiative because they commit the same mistakes: they do not take the initiative seriously, there is a lack of involvement from stakeholders, and not all the elements of DEI are taken into consideration. Some of these may include; ignoring intersectionality and inclusion, failing to provide the adequate resources for the program to progress, and, finally, a lack of accountability toward the actions.

To ensure that you do not make these mistakes, always remember to have clearly established goals and constantly monitor the metrics. This will be the thermometer that will enable you to measure what is being done and what needs improvement. The first step should be taken when you first assess the company's situation and can be followed up by carrying out additional audits.

Although these audits do not need to be performed by an external organization, by adopting this measure, you will be giving the results more credibility than just "what the HR department has to say." When concerns are voiced by external members to the organization, they help you see more clearly the reason why the initiative is not being effective.

To help you through this process, in the next chapter, I have prepared a DEI checklist for you to carry out an assessment within your company and see what the main issues you need to work on are.

# 15

# THE WORKPLACE DEI CHECKLIST

It is said that "diversity is a strength," but it's only true if the right measures are in place to create an inclusive and equitable workplace. To ensure the success of any DEI framework, organizations must evaluate their current initiatives and policies before taking action. To do this, you will need a checklist that assesses all your company departments and their current application of DEI. Knowing your current diversity profile will enable you to see where the most important measures need to be taken and where the process needs to start.

This evaluation should take place with the stakeholder and employee survey I mentioned in previous chapters. Together, they will enable you to create an action plan based on the organization's specific needs. By using the following checklist, you will be able to understand the company's "what," "why," "how," and "who," and develop a strategy.

## CONDUCTING A DEI AUDIT

Conducting a DEI audit will set the baseline for your DEI planning. The main objective of carrying out one is to give you a thorough DEI profile of your company's workplace. As an additional benefit, it will also enable you to set a market for future comparisons once you begin the DEI implementation process.

The checklist below will approach questions that must be asked on eight aspects of the company. These include, recruiting and hiring, onboarding and training development and promotion, compensation and benefits, work environment and culture, performance review and feedback process, HR policies and procedures, and offboarding. These are only a few suggestions for some of the main aspects you can approach during the assessment. Use them as a baseline to develop your own checklist and process according to your organization's demands.

## DEI CHECKLIST

### *Recruiting and Hiring*

- Are there diverse sources of talent being recruited from?
- Is the application process accessible and transparent?
- Are job descriptions inclusive and unbiased?
- Does the hiring team represent diversity in terms of gender, race, age, etc.?
- Are interviewers trained in diversity and unconscious bias?

### *Onboarding and Training*

- Are onboarding materials and programs tailored to meet the needs of diverse employees?
- Are career paths clearly defined for all employees?
- Are there enough training and development opportunities available to all employees, regardless of seniority?
- Do managers have access to DEI-focused training and resources?

- Are training sessions regarding unconscious bias and diversity conducted regularly?

***Development and Promotion***

- Is there clear criteria and objective standards for promotions?
- Are opportunities for development equally available to all employees, regardless of background or seniority level?
- Is there a transparent system in place to facilitate promotions across all departments?
- Are managers regularly encouraged to think outside the box when considering promotion opportunities?
- Are employees rewarded and lauded for their contribution to diversity initiatives?

***Compensation and Benefits***

- Are job postings transparent about salary and benefits information?
- Does the compensation structure take into account experience, merit, or performance?
- Are there any discrepancies between the pay of employees with different backgrounds (e.g., gender, race, age)?

- Are benefits offered equally to all employees regardless of background?
- Are there any policies that incentivize and reward diversity initiatives?

*Working Environment and Culture*

- Do employees feel safe and comfortable speaking up about diversity-related issues?
- Are there policies in place to prevent discrimination, harassment, and other forms of bias?
- Are teams and departments actively encouraged to collaborate to drive DEI initiatives forward?
- Does the organizational culture promote an open dialogue around differences in opinion?
- Is feedback from employees with various backgrounds regularly solicited and integrated into decision-making processes?

*Performance Review and Feedback Process*

- Are performance reviews conducted in an equitable manner, without bias toward any particular group?
- Are performance goals and objectives clearly outlined before reviews take place?

- Are there any criteria specifically aimed at evaluating progress on DEI initiatives?
- Are employees given the opportunity to provide feedback and input when their reviews are conducted?

## HR Policies and Procedures

- Are HR policies inclusive and non-discriminatory?
- Are there measures in place to protect employees from discrimination, harassment, or other forms of bias?
- Do HR procedures foster an environment where diversity is welcomed and celebrated?
- Does the organization have a policy for handling complaints about DEI issues?
- Have initiatives been taken to ensure a diverse and equitable hiring process?
- Are there clear standards for evaluating job applicants without bias?
- Do policies exist to prevent subtle forms of discrimination (e.g., microaggressions)?
- Does the organization have an internal DEI team in place, and is it regularly consulted on HR matters?

## *Offboarding*

- Are employees being given the opportunity to provide feedback before leaving the company?
- Is retention data for employees of different backgrounds regularly collected and analyzed?
- Are exit interviews conducted with departing staff to gather insights about DEI initiatives?
- Does the organization have a system in place to track offboarding trends and identify areas for improvement?
- Are there any measures in place to ensure a smooth transition for those leaving the organization?
- Are employees given the opportunity to provide feedback on diversity initiatives during their exit interview?
- Does the organization provide resources or support for staff transitioning out of the company?

Congratulations on making it this far! Now you have all the essential tools to implement a DEI program in your company. In this chapter, you have seen some of the essential questions that need to be asked when assessing your organization's current standing on DEI.

Based on these, and the employee survey, you have all the information you need to successfully develop a program tailored to your needs.

# CONCLUSION

Before you go, I want to leave you with one last story to motivate you to persist in implementing a DEI program. I want to talk about how the soda giant, Coca-Cola, created a successful diversity program by launching a talent university.

## COCA-COLA AND DEI

According to Kinloch (2020), in the beginning of the 2000s, the company felt that it lacked diversity and that the demographics were unfavorable for a company that has a global reach. To solve this problem, they launched a University Talent Program to recruit senior college students and offer them an opportunity to become part of the organization's leadership associates. These candidates would be able to specialize in several company areas in a period between two to three years.

The results for the first year were promising—candidate applications stood at 32% from people of color and 44% from women. In the second year, the result was even better as 45% of applicants declared to be people of color, while women made up a total of 54% of all applicants. The accepted candidates would undergo a mentoring program with the company's professionals and by the end of the program, most of the talent would be retained to work in the company.

Today, the company prides itself on being among the top 25 companies that have a successful DEI initiative that keeps on growing. One of the major highlights of their approach is that the strategy was woven into the organization's core values: they want their workforce to mirror their customers, eliminate inequality and biases, and use the power that their brand has to promote inclusion worldwide. They see the application of a DEI program as essential to maintaining the organization's growth and success.

Other programs that are currently ongoing under the DEI umbrella include a women's leadership council, with an objective of having a 50% female company leadership structure, by 2030. Furthermore, they provide employee inclusion networks, which are equivalent to the ERGs I had previously mentioned, they applied policies which outlined "equal work deserves equal pay," conduct analysis which is carried out by third-party experts, and publish their DEI results yearly on their website for all stakeholders to access.

As you can see, with just the start of a simple initiative, the company has managed to grow its DEI application and experience success. If you go back a few paragraphs and analyze all the steps that were taken to ensure a diverse workplace, you will see that most, if not all, the steps that I have mentioned were taken by the company —from the importance of DEI highlighted in Chapter 1, passing through the importance of employees and stakeholders, to carrying out internal audits and publishing results we saw in Chapters 12 and 15.

NOW, IT'S YOUR TURN!

Based on everything you have learned; it is now your turn to start taking the first steps. The first two things you should do is conduct an internal audit based on the checklist I provided and measure the company's "pulse" regarding DEI initiatives by listening to your employees. These will be the beginning of your new plan and strategy to start working on a DEI framework for your company.

As you go, make sure to revisit this book and use it as a reference guide to help you in case you have any questions. You can also use it to make a checklist for the steps you have implemented, for ideas on diversity initiatives, and ways to guarantee that the company's top management and C-Suite buy into the idea and provide you with the resources you need to move forward.

One thing to always keep in mind is to keep communication open. This will be one of the essential ingredients to ensure that you achieve success. Be transparent and honest about your initiatives and always ensure that you do not need to rush the process. Other organizations take years to have a full-blown program, but it all started small. I said it before and will say it again: You need to be in it for the long run and remind the decision-makers that this is a process that can take time.

If you need any support, you can always use the numbers and the information I have provided you with to back up your business case and make compelling arguments. In addition to this, I would recommend speaking to coworkers and to peers in other companies to gain personalized input on what adopting a DEI strategy meant for them and the changes they have seen. Start by providing management with numbers, training, and awareness sessions, so they can better understand where you are coming from.

If you liked this book and feel that it has helped you navigate through the challenge of implementing your DEI strategy, I invite you to leave a review or feedback on Amazon to attract other readers who might be needing help. Your opinion is much appreciated!

I wish you good luck on your journey and hope that you can soon start seeing results that will make you proud of what you have achieved.

Last but not least, trust me: You have all the knowledge you need to be a success! Trust yourself, and be confident that all you need now is support.

# REFERENCES

Achievers. (2018, January 18). *Achievers survey finds without recognition, expect employee attrition in 2018.* Achievers. https://www.achievers.com/press/achievers-survey-finds-without-recognition-expect-employee-attrition-2018/?zd_source=hrt&zd_campaign=5503&zd_term=chiradeepbasumallick

Anand, R., & Winters, M.-F. (2008). A retrospective view of corporate diversity training from 1964 to the present. *Academy of Management Learning & Education, 7*(3), 356–372. https://doi.org/10.5465/amle.2008.34251673

Andino, J. (2021, December 9). *Data & diversity: The competitive advantage of DEI.* Capital Analytics Associates. https://www.capitalanalyticsassociates.com/data-diversity-the-competitive-advantage-of-dei/

Anschutz Medical Campus. (n.d.). *Diversity, equity, & inclusion 101.* University of Colorado Denver. https://www.ucdenver.edu/offices/equity/education-training/self-guided-learning/diversity-equity-and-inclusion-101

Asare, J. G. (2020, August 30). *If you really care about equity and inclusion, stop cutting your diversity budget.* Forbes. https://www.forbes.com/sites/janicegassam/2020/08/30/if-you-really-care-about-equity-and-inclusion-stop-cutting-your-diversity-budget/?sh=50a8db424549

Axios HR. (2020, January 4). *Why workforce diversity is a huge competitive advantage.* Axios HR. https://axioshr.com/why-workforce-diversity-is-a-huge-competitive-advantage/

Baker, M. (2020, October 14). *Change fatigue is rising; first tackle small everyday changes.* Gartner. https://www.gartner.com/smarterwithgartner/how-to-reduce-the-risk-of-employee-change-fatigue

Banjoko, T. (n.d.). *Getting executive buy-in for diversity & inclusion.*

Reward Gateway. https://www.rewardgateway.com/blog/how-to-get-leadership-to-support-your-dei-initiatives

Bersin, J. (2019, March 16). *Why diversity and inclusion has become a business priority.* Josh Bersin. https://joshbersin.com/2015/12/why-diversity-and-inclusion-will-be-a-top-priority-for-2016/

Boogaard, K. (n.d.). *Nine DEI metrics you should be tracking.* Culture Amp. https://www.cultureamp.com/blog/dei-metrics

Buss, D. (2022, March 9). *Twelve ways companies are boosting their DEI.* SHRM. https://www.shrm.org/resourcesandtools/hr-topics/behavioral-competencies/global-and-cultural-effectiveness/pages/12-ways-companies-are-boosting-their-dei.aspx

Catalyst. (2018). *Why diversity and inclusion matter: Financial performance.* Catalyst. https://www.catalyst.org/research/why-diversity-and-inclusion-matter-financial-performance/

Center for Equity, Gender, and Leadership (EGAL). (n.d.). DEI (Diversity, Equity & Inclusion) Checklist level 1 -Institutional: Robust list of policies. In *Berkeley Haas.* https://haas.berkeley.edu/wp-content/uploads/EGAL_DEIChecklist.pdf

Cleland, N. (2022, April 1). *Five tried & true tips to increase stakeholder engagement with your DE&I strategy.* Flair. https://flairimpact.com/article/5-tried-true-tips-to-increase-stakeholder-engagement-with-your-dei-strategy

Cofre, R. (2022, June 3). *Embedding diversity, equity and inclusion in a corporate culture.* BenefitsPRO. https://www.benefitspro.com/2022/06/03/bettering-corporate-culture-with-dei-initiatives/?slreturn=20221127164833

Cohen, M. (2022, November 11). *Why tracking DEI initiatives and disclosing them is imperative for business.* CNBC. https://www.cnbc.com/2022/11/11/why-tracking-dei-initiatives-and-disclosing-them-is-imperative.html

Cordivano, S. (2021, April 26). *How much does diversity, equity and inclusion really cost?* Medium. https://medium.com/sarah-cordivano/how-much-does-diversity-equity-and-inclusion-really-cost-f3dae9e410f8

Corrigan, J. (2022, February 28). *Only 34% of companies have enough resources to support DEI initiatives*. Human Resources Director. https://www.hcamag.com/ca/specialization/corporate-wellness/only-34-of-companies-have-enough-resources-to-support-dei-initiatives/327171

Craig, W. (2017). *Three reasons why employee recognition will always matter*. Forbes. https://www.forbes.com/sites/williamcraig/2017/07/17/3-reasons-why-employee-recognition-will-always-matter/?sh=6da282a463c9

Crescendo. (2022, February 27). *How to build the business case for DEI at your company*. Crescendo. https://crescendowork.com/guide-start-diversity-inclusion-strategy/business-case-diversity-inclusion-company

Cross, M. (2022, January 26). *Six ways your eLearning tools can foster diversity and inclusion*. ELearning Industry. https://elearningindustry.com/ways-elearning-tools-foster-diversity-and-inclusion-dei-strategies

Culture Amp. (2022). Understanding the DEI landscape 2022. In *Culture Amp*. Culture Amp. https://www.cultureamp.com/resources/reports/2022-workplace-dei-report?

Dickson, G. (2016, June 23). *Five reasons diversity in the workplace is a competitive advantage*. Bonusly. https://blog.bonus.ly/5-competitive-benefits-of-diversity-in-the-workplace

Dillon, B., & Bourke, J. (2016). *The six signature traits of inclusive leadership-Thriving in a diverse new world*. Deloitte University Press. https://www2.deloitte.com/content/dam/Deloitte/au/Documents/human-capital/deloitte-au-hc-six-signature-traits-inclusive-leadership-020516.pdf

Diversio. (2020, October 20). *How prioritizing diversity spend can save profits*. Diversio. https://diversio.com/the-opportunity-cost-of-not-spending-on-di-2/

Dixon-Fyle, S., Dolan, K., Hunt, V., & Prince, S. (2020, May 19). *Diversity wins: How inclusion matters*. McKinsey & Company. https://www.mckinsey.com/featured-insights/diversity-and-inclusion/diversity-wins-how-inclusion-matters

Easy Llama. (n.d.). *Ten examples of unconscious bias in the workplace and how to avoid them*. Easy Llama. https://www.easyllama.com/blog/unconscious-bias-in-the-workplace/

Eightfold. (2022, August 2). *Three key features of successful DEI implementation in large organizations*. Eightfold. https://eightfold.ai/blog/successful-dei-implementation/

Electricity Human Resources. (n.d.). Diversity, equity and inclusion checklist. In *Electricity Human Resources*. https://electricityhr.ca/wp-content/uploads/2020/06/EHRC-Leadershift-Checklist-ENG.pdf

Extension Foundation. (2022). *Diversity, equity, and inclusion*. Extension Foundation. https://dei.extension.org/

Fenelon, K.-F., Mullineaux, M., & Tonti, J. (2022). *Companies are committing to DEI initiatives, but more work is needed to increase accountability and action*. JUST Capital. https://justcapital.com/reports/companies-are-committing-to-diversity-equity-and-inclusion-but-need-to-increase-accountability-and-action/

Fernandes, P. (2020, September 17). *Creating a diversity and inclusion training program*. Business News Daily. https://www.businessnewsdaily.com/9782-diversity-training.html

Forbes Expert Panel®. (2022, March 28). *Council Post: 16 t HR managers are implementing for "real" (DEI) change in the workplace*. Forbes. https://www.forbes.com/sites/forbeshumanresourcescouncil/2022/03/28/16-tips-hr-managers-are-implementing-for-real-dei-change-in-the-workplace/?sh=200213921329

Gale, S. F. (2020, December 4). *A diversity training success story*. Chief Learning Officer. https://www.chieflearningofficer.com/2020/12/04/a-diversity-training-success-story/

Garrett, C. (2022, June 28). *Why is employee recognition important in 2023?* SnackNation. https://snacknation.com/blog/why-employee-recognition-is-important/

Gebauer, M. (2021, July 29). *A lack of DEI presents serious operational, strategic, and reputational risks*. Medium. https://blog.divercity.io/a-lack-of-dei-presents-serious-operational-strategic-and-reputational-risks-643a81d4e2a3

Georgeac, O., & Rattan, A. (2022, June 15). *Stop making the business case*

# REFERENCES | 191

*for diversity*. Harvard Business Review. https://hbr.org/2022/06/stop-making-the-business-case-for-diversity

GoCo. (2022, September 18). *Ten mistakes HR pros make with DEI initiatives*. GoCo. https://www.goco.io/blog/10-mistakes-hr-pros-make-with-dei-initiatives/

Goldstein, D., Goluskin, S., Price, H., & Sperling-Magro, J. (2022, May 9). *Three steps to supercharge DE&I capability building*. McKinsey. https://www.mckinsey.com/capabilities/people-and-organizational-performance/our-insights/the-organization-blog/three-steps-to-supercharge-dei-capability-building

Gompers, P., & Kovvali, S. (2018, July). *Finally, evidence that diversity improves financial performance*. Harvard Business Review. https://hbr.org/2018/07/the-other-diversity-dividend

Gordon, A. (2022, August 17). *How can technology advance inclusion and belonging in higher education?* Includifi. https://includifi.com/blog/belonging-inclusion-edtech

Govindji, K. (2022, February 10). *Six ways to help your DEI initiatives drive greater impact*. Forbes. https://www.forbes.com/sites/googlecloud/2022/02/10/6-ways-to-help-your-dei-initiatives-driver-greater-impact/?sh=5f3febdc2eec

Gutoskey, E. (2020, June 11). *What's the difference between equity and equality?* Mental Floss. https://www.mentalfloss.com/article/625404/equity-vs-equality-what-is-the-difference

Hall, S. H. (2022, December 16). *Nine ways to measure the success of your DEI strategy in 2023*. Senior Executive. https://seniorexecutive.com/9-ways-to-measure-the-success-of-your-dei-strategy/

Hastwell, C. (2020, January 7). *What are employee resource groups (ERGs)?* Great Place to Work®. https://www.greatplacetowork.com/resources/blog/what-are-employee-resource-groups-ergs

Heinz, K. (2021, October 21). *What does DEI mean in the workplace?* Built In. https://builtin.com/diversity-inclusion/what-does-dei-mean-in-the-workplace

Hire Equal. (2020, September 29). *Hold management accountable for diversity & inclusion in the workplace*. Hire Equal. https://www.hiree

qual.com/blog/6-Tips-To-Hold-Leaders-And-Managers-Accountable-For-Building-A-Diverse-And-Inclusive-Environment

HR Covered Inc. (2021, June 11). *Seven key steps to a diverse, equitable, and inclusive workplace.* Charity Village. https://charityvillage.com/7-key-steps-to-a-diverse-equitable-and-inclusive-workplace/

HR Solutions Blog Team. (2020, August 30). *Fifteen ideas for improving diversity, equity, and inclusion.* ADP Info. https://sbshrs.adpinfo.com/blog/15-ideas-for-improving-diversity-equity-and-inclusion

Hunt, D. V., Layton, D., & Prince, S. (2015, January 1). *Why diversity matters.* Www.mckinsey.com. https://www.mckinsey.com/capabilities/people-and-organizational-performance/our-insights/why-diversity-matters

Interactive, S. (2022, July 26). *Five common DEIB strategy implementation mistakes.* Sollah. https://sollahlibrary.com/blog/five-common-dei-strategy-implementation-mistakes

Issid, J. (2011). *Have these biases been entirely rendered moot? Are companies still (consciously or otherwise) exhibiting gender favoritism during the recruiting process?* Monster Career Advice. https://www.monster.ca/career-advice/article/gender-role-during-a-job-interview-ca

JazzHR. (2021, February 9). *Four outdated HR processes - and how to fix them.* JazzHR. https://www.jazzhr.com/blog/4-outdated-hr-processes-and-how-to-fix-them/

John, A. S. (2021, November 30). *5 steps to build better internal talent pipelines.* Chief Learning Officer. https://www.chieflearningofficer.com/2021/11/30/5-steps-to-build-better-internal-talent-pipelines/

Johnson & Johnson. (2021). *Culture of inclusion | 2021 Diversity, equity & inclusion impact review.* Johnson and Johnson. https://belong.jnj.com/culture-of-inclusion

Jones, H. E. (2019). *Creating a culture of recognition.* Great Place to Work United States. https://www.greatplacetowork.com/resources/blog/creating-a-culture-of-recognition

Jung, L. (2021, August 24). *Big business pledged nearly $50 billion for racial justice after George Floyd's death. Where did the money go?* Washington

Post. https://www.washingtonpost.com/business/interactive/2021/george-floyd-corporate-america-racial-justice/

Kellogg Insight. (2020, March 2). *Yes, investors care about gender diversity.* Kellogg Insight. https://insight.kellogg.northwestern.edu/article/women-in-tech-finance-gender-diversity-investors

Kick, C. (2019, October 4). *The real cost of getting workplace diversity & inclusion wrong.* Launchways. https://www.launchways.com/the-real-cost-of-getting-workplace-diversity-inclusion-wrong/

Killermann, S. (2012). *You Soup: understanding diversity and the intersections of identity.* It's Pronounced Metrosexual. https://www.itspronouncedmetrosexual.com/2012/10/individual-difference-and-group-similiarity/

Kinloch, R. (2020, November 27). *Diverse talent: 4 influential brand stories of success.* Headstart. https://www.headstart.io/insights/diverse-talent-4-influential-brand-stories-of-success/

Kirkpatrick, J. D., & Kirkpatrick, W. (2021, October 1). *Stumped on how to measure DEI training?* TD Magazine. https://www.td.org/magazines/td-magazine/stumped-on-how-to-measure-dei-training

Kline, P. M., Rose, E. K., & Walters, C. R. (2021, July 1). *Systemic discrimination among large U.S. employers.* National Bureau of Economic Research. https://www.nber.org/papers/w29053

Lee, M., Pitesa, M., Pillutla, M. M., & Thau, S. (2018). Perceived entitlement causes discrimination against attractive job candidates in the domain of relatively less desirable jobs. *Journal of Personality and Social Psychology, 114*(3), 422–442. https://doi.org/10.1037/pspi0000114

Levine, S. R. (2020, January 15). *Diversity confirmed to boost innovation and financial results.* Forbes. https://www.forbes.com/sites/forbesinsights/2020/01/15/diversity-confirmed-to-boost-innovation-and-financial-results/?sh=11537133c4a6

LifeLabs Learning. (n.d.). *Diversity in the workplace.* LifeLabs Learning. https://www.lifelabslearning.com/blog/a-dei-audit-is-an-opportunity-to-build-community

Lorenzo, R., & Reeves, M. (2018, July 31). *How and where diversity drives financial performance*. Harvard Business Review. https://hbr.org/2018/01/how-and-where-diversity-drives-financial-performance

Lunaria Solutions. (2019). *The ROI of DEI*. Lunaria Solutions. https://lunariasolutions.com/blog-post/the-roi-of-dei/

Master Class. (2022, November 13). *Afinity bias overview: How to avoid affinity bias*. Master Class. https://www.masterclass.com/articles/affinity-bias

McConnell, B. (2021, November 2). *Ten effective ways to promote equity in the workplace*. Recruitee Blog. https://recruitee.com/articles/equity-in-workplace#5

McCormic, K. (2007). *The evolution of diversity*. NS Civic Blog; Penn State. https://sites.psu.edu/nscivicblog/2016/01/27/the-evolution-of-diversity/

McKim, J. (2021, April 20). *The business case for implementing DEI (diversity, equity and inclusion)*. NH Business Review. https://www.nhbr.com/the-business-case-for-implementing-dei-diversity-equity-and-inclusion/

McKinsey & Company. (2022). *Women in the workplace*. McKinsey. https://www.mckinsey.com/~/media/mckinsey/featured%20insights/diversity%20and%20inclusion/women%20in%20the%20workplace%202021/women-in-the-workplace-2021.pdf

McLaren, S. (2020, October 20). *Building a diverse talent pipeline: 6 meaningful steps every company can take*. LinkedIn. https://www.linkedin.com/business/talent/blog/talent-acquisition/50-plus-ideas-for-cultivating-diversity-and-inclusion

McMinn, T. (2021). *Looking back, planning forward: The history of DEI and 2022 priorities*. Lunaria. https://lunariasolutions.com/blog-post/deipriority2022/

McNamara, S. (2022, March 7). *Four ways to drive accountability for DEI in your organization*. Seramount. https://seramount.com/articles/four-ways-to-drive-accountability-for-dei-in-your-organization/

Mead, U. (2022, May 10). *Four ways to integrate DEI into your culture early on*. Forbes. https://www.forbes.com/sites/forbeshumanresourcescouncil/2022/05/10/four-ways-to-integrate-dei-into-your-culture-early-on/?sh=6d5e961c1e36

Mendez, A. (2022, August 5). *Data for diversity: How to measure your DEI performance.* Robert Half. https://www.roberthalf.com/blog/robert-half-thought-leader/data-for-diversity-how-to-measure-your-dei-performance

MentorcliQ. (2022, October 13). *What are employee resource groups? How do I start one?* MentorcliQ. https://www.mentorcliq.com/blog/what-are-employee-resource-groups-ergs

Mignot, E. (2020, May 20). *When to confront your boss? (or how to overcome authority bias?).* Medium. https://productcoalition.com/when-to-confront-your-boss-or-how-to-overcome-authority-bias-9cbd65e82810

Miller, A. (2021, September 16). *Avoiding reputation risk by embracing DEI.* Risk Management Magazine. https://www.rmmagazine.com/articles/article/2021/09/16/avoiding-reputation-risk-by-embracing-dei

Milligan, S. (2017, July 21). *Six trends that changed HR over the past decade.* SHRM; SHRM. https://www.shrm.org/hr-today/news/hr-magazine/0817/pages/6-trends-that-changed-hr-over-the-past-decade.aspx

Mind Gym. (2021, July 8). *How to get senior leadership buy-in for DE&I.* Mind Gym. https://themindgym.com/resources/articles/how-to-get-senior-leadership-buy-in-for-dei

Mobilio, L. (2019, May 10). *Empower employees to effect change - 4 Ways.* LSA Global. https://lsaglobal.com/blog/4-ways-to-inspire-and-empower-employees-to-effect-change/

Murray, L. (2019). Executive Order 880. In *Encyclopædia Britannica.* https://www.britannica.com/event/Executive-Order-8802

Nayani, F. (2022, June 2). *Are you starting an ERG? Do these 5 things.* BuiltIn. https://builtin.com/diversity-inclusion/how-to-start-an-erg

Nguyen, M. V. (2021, December 4). *Too many DEI plans are ineffective. Here are 3 ways companies can ensure progress.* Fast Company. https://www.fastcompany.com/90702054/too-many-dei-plans-are-ineffective-here-are-3-ways-companies-can-ensure-progress

Pandey, A. (2020, December 8). *Five high-impact strategies for sustaining employee behavior change*. Training Industry. https://trainingindustry.com/articles/content-development/change-employee-behavior-in-the-workplace-with-these-5-high-impact-corporate-training-strategies-spon-eidesign/

Pandey, A. (2021, November 10). *Eight key aspects that will help you create effective DEI training programs*. Training Industry. https://trainingindustry.com/articles/diversity-equity-and-inclusion/8-key-aspects-that-will-help-you-create-effective-dei-training-programs-spon-eidesign/

PayChex. (2021, September 9). *Diversity, equity & inclusion guide: How to drive value with a DEI audit*. Paychex. https://www.paychex.com/articles/human-resources/dei-audit-and-guide

Peatman, B. (2021, April 13). *How diversity is a competitive advantage*. Prialto. https://www.prialto.com/blog/how-diversity-is-a-competitive-advantage

Peralta, P. (2022, November 15). *Not investing in DEI? That decision could cost your company*. Employee Benefit News. https://www.benefitnews.com/news/what-overlooking-dei-could-cost-your-organization

Raeburn, A. (2022, July 2). *How to create an action plan that drives results*. Asana. https://asana.com/resources/action-plan

Robertson, T. (2019, March 4). *Mozilla introduces gender transitioning guidelines and policy*. Mozilla. https://blog.mozilla.org/careers/mozilla-introduces-gender-transitioning-guidelines-and-policy/

Rudd Center. (2020). *Weight bias in the workplace: Information for employers*. UConn Rudd Center for Food Policy & Obesity. https://uconnruddcenter.org/wp-content/uploads/sites/2909/2020/07/Weight-Bias-in-the-Workplace.pdf

Santos, M. (2021, July 14). *Diversity and inclusion in the workplace: 10 common mistakes*. TextExpander. https://textexpander.com/blog/diversity-and-inclusion-in-the-workplace-10-common-mistakes

Schoenhoff, B. (2021, July 6). *Building a culture of diversity, equity & inclusion (DEI) at work*. GoCo. https://www.goco.io/blog/building-culture-of-dei-at-work/

Seen at Work Team. (2022, June 4). *Employee resource groups: How to unlock the full potential of ERGs*. Seen at Work. https://www.seenat work.com/insights/employee-resource-groups

SHRM. (2021, May 19). *Introduction to the human resources discipline of diversity, equity and inclusion*. SHRM. https://www.shrm.org/resourcesandtools/tools-and-samples/toolkits/pages/introdiversity.aspx

Shufeldt, J. (2021, August 28). *The importance of DEI*. LinkedIn. https://www.linkedin.com/pulse/importance-dei-john-shufeldt-md-jd-mba-facep/

Stembridge, G. (2020, October 30). *How to build the business case for your DEI strategy*. Qualtrics. https://www.qualtrics.com/blog/build-a-dei-strategy/

Survey Monkey. (n.d.). *How to measure DEI in the workplace*. Survey Monkey. https://www.surveymonkey.com/mp/mp-measuring-dei/

Terkel. (2022). *Ten DE&I leaders "pass the torch": 10 things you can do to personally make a change*. Texthelp. https://www.texthelp.com/resources/blog/10-dei-leaders-pass-the-torch-10-things-you-can-do-to-personally-make-a-change/

Todd-Ryan, S. (2019, May 5). *Why diversity gives businesses a competitive advantage*. Forbes. https://www.forbes.com/sites/samanthatodd/2019/05/05/the-business-case-for-diversity-a-competitive-advantage/?sh=56357d995a1b

Tolbert, R. (2020, November 18). *Are you making these 5 common workplace diversity, equity and inclusion mistakes?* Great Place to Work®. https://www.greatplacetowork.com/resources/blog/5-diversity-and-inclusion-mistakes

Urwin, M. (2019). *The cold, hard truth about ageism in the workplace*. Built In. https://builtin.com/diversity-inclusion/ageism-in-the-workplace

van Vulpen, E. (2022, February 1). *Ten DEI metrics your organization should track*. AIHR. https://www.aihr.com/blog/dei-metrics/

Visier. (n.d.). *Four steps to building a business case for DEI*. Visier. https://www.visier.com/blog/4-steps-to-building-a-business-case-for-diversity-and-inclusion/

Vozza, S. (2020, August 7). *Avoid these 8 common mistakes when creating a*

D&I policy. Fast Company. https://www.fastcompany.com/90537483/avoid-these-8-common-mistakes-when-creating-a-di-policy

VSource. (2020, August 3). *The evolution of diversity in the workplace - 2000 to 2020.* VSource. https://www.vsource.io/blog/evolution-of-diversity-in-the-workplace

Vulpen, E. van. (2022, February 1). *Ten DEI metrics your organization should track.* AIHR. https://www.aihr.com/blog/dei-metrics/#Demographics

Ward, M. (2020, March 4). *C-suite leaders are making a big assumption about their workforce — and it's bleeding the economy of $1.05 trillion.* Business Insider. https://www.businessinsider.com/accenture-report-perception-gap-shows-economic-cost-lack-of-diversity-inclusion

Waters, S. (2021, June 17). *What is an employee resource group and why do they matter?* Better Up. https://www.betterup.com/blog/employee-resource-group

Weisenfeld, D. (2022, March 30). *Eight steps for using data to improve workforce DEI.* Work Design Magazine. https://www.workdesign.com/2022/03/eight-steps-for-using-data-to-improve-workforce-dei/

WellRight. (2022, March 15). *Getting past the top 5 barriers to DEI program implementation.* WellRight. https://www.wellright.com/blog/getting-past-top-5-barriers-dei-program-implementation

Wickham, N. (2021, June 10). *The importance of employee recognition: Statistics and research.* Quantum Workplace. https://www.quantumworkplace.com/future-of-work/importance-of-employee-recognition

Williams, S. (2020, February 25). *Evolution of diversity in the workplace.* LinkedIn. https://www.linkedin.com/pulse/evolution-diversity-workplace-stacey-williams/

Wilson, R. (2021, February 25). *Unconscious bias in the workplace: how it's defined and how to stop it.* EW Group. https://theewgroup.com/blog/unconscious-bias-in-the-workplace-how-its-defined-and-how-to-stop-it/

Winder, J. (2022, August 1). *Introducing DEI in the workplace*. LinkedIn. https://www.linkedin.com/pulse/introducing-dei-workplace-shrl-cmhr-sphr-shrm-scp/?trk=pulse-article

Woo, E. (2019, October 25). *Autism at work: Encouraging neurodiversity in the workplace*. SAP News Center. https://news.sap.com/2019/10/workplace-neurodiversity-autism-at-work-program/

World Economic Forum. (2020). Diversity, equity and inclusion 4.0—A toolkit for leaders to accelerate social progress in the future of work. In *World Economic Forum*. https://www3.weforum.org/docs/WEF_NES_DEI4.0_Toolkit_2020.pdf

Wronski, L. (2021). *CNBC/SurveyMonkey workforce happiness index: April 2021*. SurveyMonkey. https://www.surveymonkey.com/curiosity/cnbc-workforce-survey-april-2021/

Xu, T. (2019). *Twelve unconscious bias examples and how to avoid them in the workplace*. Built In. https://builtin.com/diversity-inclusion/unconscious-bias-examples

Young, F. (n.d.). *Eleven step approach to creating a more inclusive culture*. Hive Learning. https://www.hivelearning.com/site/resource/diversity-inclusion/create-an-inclusive-culture-at-scale/

Printed in Great Britain
by Amazon